PRAISE FOR THE CLASSICAL MARKETING BOOK

"The head of Shell's recruitment department was once asked why the company hired so many classics graduates. His answer: 'We find that they sell more oil.' Reading this book, we can better understand why. Tas's book proves that classics can indeed help us in today's marketing world, provided we can still find time to blend ancient wisdom with contemporary relevance."

RORY SUTHERLAND
VICE CHAIR, OGILVY GROUP

"An intriguing journey into the world of myths, memories and the power of persuasion. Tas explores the wisdom of Homer, Aristotle, Cicero – and, of course, the Sugababes. The Classical Marketing Book is 'classic Tas': mixing useful insights and practical tips with clever wordplay and the occasional dad joke. If you've read one of his books before then you'll know what's coming – if not, then it's probably time to find out!"

ANDY BURRELL
HEAD OF PORTFOLIO MARKETING, CNS, NOKIA

"'No new thing under the sun.' In his latest book, Tas takes a leaf out of Ecclesiastes, and traces lessons, inspirations and cautionary tales from the ancient worlds of Greece and Rome. Myths and misses, strategies and stratagems – Tas shows how each can open doors and shut down blind alleys in today's world. Buy a copy and start crossing some of your own Rubicons."

RICHARD SWAAB

"In Tas's latest book, he presents an intriguing perspective on how classical literature and mythology can improve modern marketing. Who would have thought that the timeless wisdom of the classics could provide contemporary marketers with insights into thinking and communication? This book is a delightful surprise, proving that classics can indeed be fun and relevant in today's fast-paced marketing world.

At the heart of the book is the theme of storytelling. Tas argues that effective messaging is rooted in the art of narrative, and this is where the literary toolkit of classical myths comes into play. By integrating elements of Greek mythology with modern storytelling techniques, including fun references to popular TV shows like Game of Thrones, the book illustrates how marketers can craft compelling stories that resonate with their audiences.

Overall, The Classical Marketing Book *is a refreshing take on marketing communication, blending ancient wisdom with contemporary relevance. It challenges readers to think critically and creatively, serving as a valuable resource for anyone looking to improve their messaging. Whether you're a seasoned marketer or just starting out, this book will transform the way you approach your craft."

PETER HAIGH
CHAIR, MINTEL

"What a joyful, fast-paced and highly inspirational read The Classical Marketing Book is. Lovers of language will feast on Tas's etymological delights. This is a bouncy, witty and word-crafted exploration of the lessons that marketers can learn from the classics. Bouncy because one genuinely never knows what's coming one the next page, which is a good thing if one likes discovery. Witty because ... well, Tas is a genuinely funny man and sees dry humour everywhere. Word-crafted is a dreadful adjective (sorry, Tas) but the book is so beautifully written that it's a joy to soak in every sentence."

DOM HAWES
GROUP CEO, SELBEY ANDERSON

"This is truly unlike any other marketing book I have ever read! (In the best possible way, I hasten to add).

The book provides a witty and very accessible gateway to the core mythologies and theories that strive to make sense of the human condition. Tas eloquently, and often humorously, takes the thoughts of these great thinkers and reframes them for the modern marketer, reminding us that there is more to this profession than clicks and followers.

It takes the lesser-seen Venn diagram of an expert classicist and a seasoned marketer to meander effortlessly from Cicero to the Sugababes via Aristotle, Jeff Goldblum, Mark Zuckerberg and Quintilian."

RACHEL MACEY
MD, KANTAR MEDIA

"A masterclass in storytelling from a classicist, marketing/comms expert and a great wordsmith to boot. This book will renew your love of communications and give you easy-to-implement steps to breathe new life into your brand. Drawing lessons from the classics and applying them to the modern business world of communications should feel harder than this. Tas once again displays his flair for making the complex simple. This book is so easy to digest, it almost reads itself, and I found myself literally laughing out loud."

AINE GIRN
HEAD OF MARKETING, S JONES CONTAINERS

"In this inspirational and charming gem, the indefatigable Tasgal this time casts his eye on the origins of enduring best practice in persuasion and presentation from the wisdom of the classical world. Seize this book and seize the day."

JUSTIN HOLLOWAY
HEAD OF STRATEGY, EUROPE, SYNEOS HEALTH

"Forget stale strategy decks and jargon-laced brand pyramids. This is marketing with a toga on and a sharp tongue in its cheek.

In this brilliant and bold guide, Tas Tasgal draws on the ancient worlds of Greece and Rome to breathe new life into modern marketing. He shows how mythology fuels memorable branding, why dead languages can sharpen your copy and how classical rhetoric can give your persuasion power and punch.

Entertaining, insightful and totally unlike your average business book, this is for anyone who wants to swap clichés for clarity and rediscover the timeless art of influence. Whether you're a CMO, creative, copywriter or consultant, this book will challenge how you think, speak and persuade.

Classics never go out of style."

JOHN QUINN
HEAD OF INSIGHT, PHOENIX GROUP/STANDARD LIFE

FOR OTHER TITLES IN THE SERIES ...

CLEVER CONTENT, DYNAMIC IDEAS, PRACTICAL SOLUTIONS AND ENGAGING VISUALS – A CATALYST TO INSPIRE NEW WAYS OF THINKING AND PROBLEM-SOLVING IN A COMPLEX WORLD

www.lidpublishing.com/product-category/concise-advice-series

Published by
LID Publishing
An imprint of LID Business Media Ltd.
LABS House, 15-19 Bloomsbury Way,
London, WC1A 2TH, UK

info@lidpublishing.com
www.lidpublishing.com

A member of:

businesspublishersroundtable.com

All rights reserved. Without limiting the rights under copyright reserved, no part of this publication may be reproduced, stored or introduced into a retrieval system, or transmitted, in any form or by any means (electronic, mechanical, photocopying, recording or otherwise) without the prior written permission of both the copyright owners and the publisher of this book.

© Anthony Tasgal, 2025
© LID Business Media Limited, 2025

Printed and bound in Great Britain by Halstan Ltd

ISBN: 978-1-915951-78-6
ISBN: 978-1-915951-79-3 (ebook)

Cover and page design: Caroline Li

THE CLASSICAL MARKETING BOOK

MARKETING LESSONS FROM THE GREEKS AND ROMANS

ANTHONY TASGAL

MADRID | MEXICO CITY | LONDON
BUENOS AIRES | BOGOTA | SHANGHAI

CONTENTS

INTRODUCTION: IT AIN'T OEUVRE TILL IT'S OEUVRE   2
- Dead languages   4
- A digression: on hedgehogs and foxes   11
- Structure: the book as a whole is divided into three parts   18

PART ONE: MYTHOLOGY   22
- On the timelessness of myth: "now these things never happened, but always are"   26
- Foundation myths   30
- Brand mythologies   32
- Adapting, co-opting and reframing myths   44
- Why myth matters   49
- A segmented mythology of mythic characters   51
- Do the myth   66
- Implications and insights (cui bono?)   67

PART TWO: VOCABULARY   70
- Authority   72
- Character   74
- Acronymous fish   77
- Putting the meta in metaphysics   81
- Theseus, meet the Sugababes   83

- Information ... 87
- Symbolon: going ballistic ... 89
- Jump Around ... 91
- Decide: cutting down our choices ... 94
- A tenth situation ... 96
- Thumbs up or down? ... 97
- Kosmos: the final frontier ... 99
- No business of yours ... 101
- Be more Caesar ... 103
- Finally and unexpectedly ... 108
- Cui bono: insights ... 112

PART THREE: PERSUASION ... 118
- Rhetorically speaking ... 120
- The origins of rhetoric: 3 + 4 = 7 ... 123
- Ethics and persuasion ... 125
- I'm spinning around (apologies to Kylie) ... 127
- It's benign o'clock ... 130
- Lawyering up ... 132
- A little sophistication ... 134
- Cicero and the five canons ... 136

PERORATIO ... 152
- Stealing a moment ... 154
- *Locus classicus* ... 156
- *In fine* ... 158
- The modern trivium ... 164

ENDNOTES ... 168
ACKNOWLEDGEMENTS ... 179
ABOUT THE AUTHOR ... 180

To all the great classical educators,
especially Nigel, Mary, Bettany and Natalie

INTRODUCTION:
IT AIN'T OEUVRE TILL IT'S OEUVRE

So, welcome to another entry in the oeuvre – book seven.

I thought I should start with a few words about where this title fits in, for those of you who have already got to the question "Why spend my hard-earned cash on a book about Aristotle and Cicero to learn how to talk to Swiftie fashion influencers?"

When penning the delightfully termed 'advance praise' for my previous book (*The Consumer Behaviour Book*), one of my clients, the lovely Klynn Alibocus then of Boehringer Ingelheim, suggested there might be an order to reading my books. Start with *The Consumer Behaviour Book*, he recommended, then move on to *The Insight Book* and then *The Storytelling Book*.

Fair enough.

So, where does this work fit into the oeuvre, the scheme of things?

I would suggest that alongside *InCitations*, it is part of my broader mission to make marketing and business generally more porous to ideas and influences that don't occur naturally in the typical business habitat. Just as *The Consumer Behaviour Book* featured behavioural economics – as well as offering a body of principles and theory for understanding how decisions are made, and how to influence them – it was also intended as a welcome external shot in the arm for the business world, as behavioural economics emerged largely unheralded from the academic environment.

We need more of this. The entire argument of *The Insight Book* (some may call it a Golden Thread) was that the engine of insight (or, if you prefer, creativity and originality) is connection and serendipity.

And one of my enduring themes from *The Inspiratorium* to *InCitations* to *The Insight Book* is that insight, novelty, creativity – call it what you will – comes from creating something in the brain that evokes a sense of what Isaac Asimov defined as a feeling of "that's funny …"[1]

This has been one of my guiding principles, and I wanted to extend that tenet (Latin for 'it holds') here.

So, where better to look for a way to inject fresh blood and insight into the senescent body of marketing understanding than in the worlds of classical Greece and Rome?

DEAD LANGUAGES

For those naysayers who presumably aren't reading this anyway as they've chosen to spend their hypothetical bitcoinage on, maybe, another book on social media that will be outdated by the time they open it, I would point to the vibrancy of the classical world as we find ourselves in the mid-2020s.

At the time of writing in spring 2025, I can point to the Netflix series *Kaos* (2024–), with Jeff Goldblum perfectly cast as Zeus in a contemporary reimagining of Greek mythology. Netflix also features a French gangster series *Furies* (2024–), as well as a German sci-fi thriller, *Cassandra* (2025–), and a "steamy, sexy" Colombian thriller, *Medusa* (2025–). Then there is *Those About to Die* (2024–), a Roman epic of sports rivalries with Anthony Hopkins as Emperor Vespasian.

Or look at the success of Stephen Fry's Greek Myths series – *Mythos*, *Heroes*, *Troy* and *Odyssey* (2017–2024) – as well as many other tellings or retellings.

Recent years have also seen an outpouring of such Homeric reimaginings and fillings-out as David Malouf's novel *Ransom* (2009), based on book 24 of Homer's *The Iliad*, and Zachary Mason's extraordinary reimaginings in *The Lost Books of the Odyssey* (2007), in which he devised untold imaginings of hypothetical narratives for the wandering Odysseus. There is also Madeline Miller's *Song of Achilles* (2011), featuring the boyhoods of Patroclus and Achilles, and *Circe* (2018). And that is without mentioning Jennifer Saint's *Ariadne* (2021) and *Hera* (2024); Pat Barker's trilogy of Greek war stories, ending in *The Voyage Home* (2024); the mini library of classicist-stand-up Natalie Haynes; and Margaret Atwood's *The Penelopiad*, a feminist retelling of *The Odyssey*.

The latest author to reshape classical Greek myths is Mark Haddon (of *The Curious Incident of the Dog in the Night-Time* fame). His latest collection of short stories, *Dogs and Monsters* (2024), reconfigures and reshapes Greek myths from the Minotaur (told largely from the perspective of his grieving mother, Pasiphaë) to Actaeon, turned into a stag and ravaged by his own dogs, to the love affair between the beautiful youth Tithonus and Eos, goddess of the dawn.

Or the Irish writer Ferdia Lennon's rambunctious debut novel, *Glorious Exploits* (2024), set in 412 BC, as the Peloponnesian War rages and the Sicilian city of Syracuse has been "turned inside out and on its head" by a failed Athenian invasion.[2]

Various theatre productions of *Oedipus* (billed as "after Sophocles") are being staged in London's West End, as well as a version of Sophocles' *Elektra* (featuring Brie Larson). There is also a musical re-imagining of Orpheus and Eurydice, *Hadestown*.

TV has also recently featured *Domina* (2021–2023), two seasons detailing the story of Livia Drusilla, wife of the Roman emperor

Augustus, and *Britannia* (2018-2021), created by Jez Butterworth and set during the Roman invasion of Britain in 43 CE. Both followed in the sandal steps of the 1970s series based on Robert Graves's novel *I, Claudius* (1934) and the TV series *Rome* (2005-2007). And there is also "Rome: Total War" (2004).

Hollywood has given us films such as *Troy* (2004), Oliver Stone's *Alexander* (2004) and *300: Rise of an Empire* (2014).

And 2024 saw the return of cinematic titan Francis Ford Coppola with *Megalopolis* (Greek for 'big city'). In the director's words, it was a dream script, though some critics felt it was more of a vanity project, given it was 40 years in the making, required Coppola to sell one of his wineries to finance it and allegedly involved over 300 rewrites. A Roman epic set in modern America, it transposes the (true) story of the Catiline conspiracy to overthrow the Roman Republic in 63 BCE, under the consulship of Cicero, into a sci-fi future. The Roman references are explicit: the city is called New Rome, Adam Driver's character is (rather confusingly) called Cesar Catalina, and Giancarlo Esposito (*Breaking Bad*'s Gus Fring) is the mayor, Franklyn Cicero.

Then there is a regular stream of articles and TV documentaries from the likes of Bettany Hughes, Michaels Wood and Scott, art critic Alastair Sooke, and retired Cambridge don Dame Mary Beard (now rightfully recognized well beyond her penchant for glamorous footwear). TV also never tires, thankfully, of showcasing the latest finds in Pompeii, such as in the BBC's mini-series *Pompeii: The New Dig* (2024-2025).

A reminder of our eternal fascination with Vesuvius's 79 CE deluge (for Pompeii nerds, it's never too early to use the term 'pyroclastic surge') came when a fresco was found depicting what was generally considered by the experts to be a plate of focaccia, fruit and a goblet of wine. But this was enough to tempt some experts into posting that this was the first depiction of ... a pizza.

The pizza frenzy was slightly muted by the observation that there was neither tomato nor mozzarella (they were only introduced to Europe from the Americas in the 18th century), and the depiction of what looked like a pineapple contributed to the divisive debate around its presence on any pizza ever.

(Correct answer: never.)

The pizza PR industry went full pizzazz, and the art of the Neapolitan pizzamaker was put on UNESCO's Intangible Cultural Heritage List in 2017.[3]

In other classically related beverage news, in 2022 Starbucks launched an Odyssey coffee blend ("with notes of grapefruit nectar," for those who know and care more about coffee than I do).[4] I did propose a new variant named after the one-eyed Cyclops, Polyphemus, called The Odyssey Blind, but have yet to hear back from Seattle.

Starbucks have history here (ancient?) in that they once labelled their Caesar salad 'I, Caesar' in a knowing nod, one assumes, to Robert Graves.

This prompts me to imagine the following hypothetical conversation in front of the Roman Forum in 44 BCE:

> Brutus: Have you seen the new 'I, Caesar' wrap at Starbucks, o Cassius?
> Cassius: Yes, they look tasty.
> Brutus: So, have you tried one yet?
> Cassius: Yes, in fact I ate two, Brute.

(I am also working on a Greek epic poetry sitcom called Hi, Honey, I'm Homer. *Perhaps featuring Achillean Murphy in the main role.)*

And there are constant echoes of classical names. When we see Czar or Kaiser in history books, we are seeing a palimpsest ('etched again') of the cognomen (family name) of Julius Caesar.

The name Sasha/Sacha seems to be enjoying its time in the zeitgeist limelight, with holders ranging from Barack Obama's daughter to comedian Sacha Baron Cohen to 1960s French crooner Sacha Distel to a host of Croatian, Serbian and Macedonian sportspeople, and even German tennis player Sascha Zverev. It is also the forename of characters in the British soaps *Holby City* (1999-2022) and *EastEnders* (1985-), and the name singer Lizzo gave to her flute.

Of personal interest is that many believe the Dutch name Saskia (my daughter's name) may come from the same root.

Sasha/Sacha is a unisex diminutive of Alexander, especially common in Slavic cultures and a living legacy of Alexander of Macedon (aka 'the Great'). It derives etymologically from the words 'protector of mankind.'

Finally, someone else known for his longstanding fascination with Rome: Meta-Head, Mark Zuckerberg. His interest began when he studied classics at prep school. He is known to be enthralled by Rome and Latin, even admitting to a man crush on Emperor Augustus: two of his children are named August and Aurelia, after two of the Roman emperors.[5]

In September 2024, at Meta's annual Connect conference, Zuckerberg took to the stage in a T-shirt bearing the message 'Aut Zuck Aut Nihil' ('either Zuck or nothing'), a typically humble reference to 'Aut Caesar Aut Nihil,' associated with Cesare Borgia (it doesn't seem to belong to the era of the Roman Republic).[6]

This wasn't the first time Zuckerberg had worn a shirt with a bold message. For his 40th birthday, he donned a shirt that read 'Carthago delenda est,' meaning 'Carthage must be destroyed,' a reference to Rome's ancient enmity with Carthage and associated with Cato the Elder.[7]

And lastly, the political arena has seen plenty of Greek references, especially to the idea of a 'kakistocracy.' This admittedly niche term – meaning 'rule by the worst,' as opposed to 'aristocracy,' signifying 'rule by (those deemed to be) the best' – became something of a meme in late 2024 referring to Donald J. Trump's cabinet.[8]

DISCLAIMER

Anyone who has watched the cult UK sitcom *Peep Show*, which ran from 2003 to 2015 and featured two dysfunctional friends, Mark Corrigan and Jeremy Usbourne, sharing a flat in Croydon in South London, may recall a book that Mark tries to publish, titled *Business Secrets of the Pharaohs*.

I hope this book doesn't fall into the same trap as Mark's tome, which claims that it "makes irresistible connections between figures such as Mentuhotep V and Richard Branson" or replicates the fact that the publisher ('British London') spells Mark's surname wrong on the cover (along with the word 'Pharaohs').

(You can even purchase a meticulously recreated replica, including the typos, or visit Mark's LinkedIn page.)

A DIGRESSION:
ON HEDGEHOGS AND FOXES

Archilochus was a lyric poet of the 7th century BCE, and was so revered by the ancient commentators as to be worthy of being mentioned in the same breath as the incomparable Hesiod and Homer. Sadly, most of his work is now lost, but some tantalizing fragments remain.

One is an epigram:

> A fox knows many things, but a hedgehog [just] one big thing.

This quote has enjoyed quite some longevity as a result of the 20th-century Russian-British philosopher Isaiah Berlin, who used it as the basis for an essay, largely about the Russian novelist Leo Tolstoy.[9]

In so doing, he constructed an enduring and potent metaphorical spectrum on which to locate great thinkers, and by which to position ourselves as speakers, persuaders and thought leaders.

In Berlin's reframing, a hedgehog is the deviser and guardian of 'one big idea,' a unique lens through which to view and understand the world – so Berlin includes the likes of Plato, Nietzsche and Proust in this category.

These days we might add, for example, the three great iconoclasts Freud (whose big idea is the existence and power of the unconscious), Marx (the role and potential of class) and Darwin (the theory of evolution by natural selection).

Present-day examples include Richard Dawkins (the gene-centred view of evolution), Thomas Piketty (the distribution of money) or even the recently deceased Daniel Kahneman (the importance of the irrational in decision-making).

The dream of the hedgehog is what scientists call a GUT or a TOE (for some reason, body parts loom large in the imagery of cosmologists and physicists): a 'grand unified theory' or a 'theory of everything.'

This was the vision of the likes of Einstein and those who sought to reconcile quantum physics and relativity.

If hedgehogs are top-down seekers of the one big idea, foxes, on the other hand, are more eclectic and less reductionist, always aware that not everything can be subsumed into one neat categorization. For Berlin, foxes covered anyone from Aristotle to Shakespeare to James Joyce.

Thinking about my previous books, I would suggest that each fits neatly into one category.

Four are hedgehog books:

- *The Storytelling Book* and *The Storytelling Workbook*: the neglect of the power of storytelling in so much present-day communication results from worshipping 'arithmocracy'

- *The Insight Book:* insight does not just emerge from staring long and longingly at data, but is a creative pursuit

- *The Consumer Behaviour Book*: following Kahneman, in our behaviour change communications we must acknowledge and address the emotions and the power of unconscious (System 1) thinking[10]

The other two are fox books:

- *The Inspiratorium*: why insight comes from making new, serendipitous connections and many ways of making that happen

- *InCitations*: an eclectic collection of sayings, maxims and slogans that can generate new ways of thinking

THINKING OUTSIDE THE FOX

Berlin's metaphor has survived and thrived in Darwinian fashion, and many heirs have adopted and adapted his idea.

Philip E. Tetlock, professor of political psychology at the University of Pennsylvania, has used Berlin's hedgehog-fox spectrum to explore the success rates of experts and forecasters. The world benefits from both hedgehogs and foxes. Tetlock argues that if you are looking for accurate forecasts, you will do better to employ foxes.[11]

The psephologist and forecaster Nate Silver also used the spectrum, with reference to Tetlock, in his book *The Signal and The Noise*.[12] Indeed, Silver loved the idea of being a fox so much that he used it as the logo of his political blog fivethirtyeight.com (now under ABC News), and Fivey Fox even has its own X (previously Twitter) account (of course it does).

Operating in a similar field are John Kay and former Bank of England governor Mervyn King. In their book *Radical Uncertainty*, they describe decision-making for an unknowable future. (I especially appreciate their focus on storytelling in economics, as well as their support of what they call "evolutionary rationality.")[13]

What is so refreshing is their fox-like acceptance of puzzles, mysteries and what Donald Rumsfeld famously called "unknown unknowns" (sometimes amusingly abbreviated as 'unk-unks'). For hedgehogs, such uncertainties and loose ends are to be disregarded.

THE FOX MINDSET

Carol Dweck's work, summarized in her book *Mindset*, has enjoyed great acclaim and become almost its own cliché.[14]

Dweck argues that the notion of personality as fixed is a big part of the reason we suffer from stress, anxiety and lack of success. Many of us, she says, carry around a "fixed mindset," the implicit belief that our abilities are pre-set. This triggers anxiety as we feel we must live up to our innate abilities, and causes us to avoid new challenges in case they exceed our pre-set challenges.

Instead, we should adopt a growth mindset: and see our self as perpetually changing, adapting and in flux rather than the who you have been and will remain.

THE RESEARCH AND INSIGHT FOX

One application I have for Archilochus relates to a world I know well: that of data, research and insight analysis.

TWO APPROACHES

DATA AS CONFIRMATION		DATA AS DIRECTIVE	
+	**−**	**+**	**−**
• FAST-MOVING • INVOLVING • FRAMEWORK • MORE WOOD THAN TREES	• GETS FIXED TOO EARLY? • TOO COMMITTED? • NOT COMING TO TERMS WITH ALL INFORMATION?	• THOROUGH • LOGICAL • 'TEXTBOOK' WAY • ... FOR THOSE WHO WISH TO IMMERSE	• TAKES TIME • MORE TREES THAN WOOD • CAN LEAD TO LACK OF FOCUS

FIGURE 1

What is the best way to approach the analysis and distillation of data and research? Is it better to be a hedgehog or a fox – or is there a third way? Is there an optimal cognitive style?

On the left in *Figure 1* is the Way of the Hedgehog. This involves starting with a confirmed view, a big idea or a hypothesis that may be held with various strengths of conviction. That way, the brain looks at and explores the data to confirm or – this is essential – possibly disconfirm or disprove the hypothesis (otherwise, confirmation bias can run rampant). For many this style appeals, as it works with the brain's tendency to start with, or look for, a story. The hedgehog is most at home with the big picture – the wood rather than the trees.

On the right is the Vulpine Way. Rather than going in all guns blazing with an expectation, hypothesis or story, the fox lets the data guide them before coming to any rash conclusions. They approach the data thoroughly, careful not to ignore the wider wood but to delve among the trees.

So, if it's not too facile, perhaps this is an example of different approaches that suit different individuals differently.

But at least, if you find yourself naturally veering too unswervingly into one of the categories, you can catch yourself doing so, and adjust accordingly.

BRUTAL HEDGEHOGS

From my years in the advertising world, I recall a maxim of M&C Saatchi that reduced the principle of creativity to one brutally simplistic thought: the "brutal simplicity of thought."[15]

At the time and subsequently when it inevitably became a book, I recall thinking this was the Hedgehog's Hedgehog.

Yes, in the communications world, a big idea or an insight (see *The Insight Book*) can be genuinely transformative and maybe even 'change the world.' And readers of my other books will know that I generally espouse simplicity (it's even an acronym for my storytelling training).

But to require every idea be *that* brutally simplistic (at one point the Saatchis demanded that a brand be reduced to one word) can become unnecessarily and sweepingly reductionist.

FOR FOX SAKE

So, I would like to think of this book as a space for foxes: those scrappy, eclectic hunters who thrive on working from the bottom up, building nests and thoughts from the nuances, nudges and incidental insights they find.

One final recommendation, for those in HR supporting work in insight and creativity. Perhaps the ideal team is one composed equally of foxes and hedgehogs, or those who have a foot (paw?) in each camp.

Nuance and subtlety versus one (potentially overly simplistic) organizing principle.

STRUCTURE:
THE BOOK AS A WHOLE IS DIVIDED INTO THREE PARTS

Anyone with an elementary education in Latin will undoubtedly (and, in some cases, painfully) recognize the allusion, from Caesar (J)'s propaganda-friendly account of his time conquering Gaul, generally translated as *Commentaries on the Gallic Wars* (which lasted from 58 to 50 BCE).

Historians study it for its insight into what Caesar did (or said he did) during the Roman annexation of Gaul; for those entering the hallowed corridors of Latin, it acts as a gentle introduction to the joys of translating the language's prose. To add some historical context, those same historians (inevitably) disagree, but a figure of 1 million Gauls/Celts killed and a similar number enslaved is considered not implausible.[16]

As well as being recognized and taught because of its concise, stripped-back prose, Caesar's Gallic memoir has the benefit of beginning with the blandly memorable "Gaul as a whole is divided into three parts."

(This, I reckon, is appropriately the third book in which I have discussed the power of three.)

Fans of the *Astérix and Obélix* comic books will also be familiar with all this, and are regularly and generously rewarded with allusions to Caesar and the Gallic Wars (given it's the subject and setting of the books) – for example, when JC refers to himself in the third person (as he does throughout the *Commentaries*). And we will see more of Caesar's aphorisms later (such as the idea of 'crossing the Rubicon').

This practice of referring to oneself in the third person has – of course – a name: illeism. And famous illeists include Elmo, Richard Nixon, Salvador Dalí and Donald J. Trump. Draw your own conclusions.[17]

So, Tas will now outline his tripartite structure for the book. And, to set your mind at ease, no Gauls were harmed during the writing of it.

THE THREE PARTS: MVP OR MVP?

Some people might call it a Golden Thread (do I have to explain?), but here is the coherent structure or framework for what lies ahead, conveniently summarized in the acronym MVP.

Your understanding of this acronym will depend on whether you approach it from a business or sporting point of view. You may immediately associate it with 'minimum viable product,' a real or hypothetical product created with the least effort or fewest essential features to test the core idea before tweaks can be made.

Or you may think of sport (especially in the US), where it means 'most valuable player' (a largely self-descriptive term, so further elaboration is pointless).

My own version of MVP is as follows: mythology, vocabulary and persuasion/propaganda.

- **Mythology**: What can we learn from the history and myths of ancient Greece and Rome, and how can we absorb, adapt and employ them in our communications as analogies, metaphors and Golden Threads?

- **Vocabulary**: How can a dip into etymology and the linguistic thesaurus (originally a Greek word for a storehouse of treasure) of Greek and Latin help us become more memorable and effective communicators, from words and expressions that just make us – or our audience – think differently to new ways of thinking and framing by moving beyond much of the meaningless jargon and cliché we surround ourselves with?

- **Persuasion/propaganda**: For those of you reading this who are in the persuasion, influence or coercion business (so that's all of you), the ancients had much to teach us about the art and science of persuasion, be it rhetoric, oratory or behaviour change.

So, I have three (inevitably) broad goals here:

1. Help you avoid the meaningless depths of jargon by revitalizing your well of linguistic inspiration, for your presentations, documents, speeches and pitches.

2. Introduce some new (and/or old) ideas that can pep up and add insight to the way you think about or frame your arguments and tell your stories, be it for your brand, your comms or your CV/LinkedIn profile.

3. Enable you to learn – or relearn – lessons from the great thinkers on persuasion and influence and apply them to your company, brand, communications, speeches, etc. in order to impart more of a sense of wonder.

> **Myths always take wings and soar beyond the place where we can keep them fixed.**

Ben Okri[18]

PART **ONE**

MYTHOLOGY

If you want me to be your mentor and take you on a titanic Odyssey, make sure you don't lose your thread or get infected by a Trojan horse – in case you open up a veritable Pandora's box.

Know yourself – otherwise that might be your Achilles heel, and then you might find yourself caught in colossal chaos between Scylla and Charybdis without an atlas, distracted by the siren call of other so-called sophists or maybe trapped in a labyrinth of erotic desires (platonic or otherwise), tempted by the lure of aphrodisiacs on Amazon. Bereft of a eureka moment, you might get sour grapes.

So, don't panic: it may be a Herculean task, if not a marathon, and I won't hector or tantalize you, but I'll grab the bull by its horns, and help you to lick things into shape. Oh, and carpe that diem …

As someone fascinated by the communicative power of storytelling (see books various), I want to explore the power of stories and myths and how we can use them to feed into what my publisher once called my "life's mission": to make our communications more memorable and effective.

Myths are stories we tell ourselves to explain the world. They are a timeless body of fundamental wisdom, the encapsulation of philosophy in story form, the embodiment of urges, instincts and fears. They don't have to be finite or complete like stories, but can branch out, intersect and fly off fancifully in wild abandon.

Ancient myths provide a core of human wisdom that can not only help us live better lives but also provide an infinite bounty of ideas, metaphors and analogies for any form of communication, professional or private, as well as educate us in the moral and philosophical realms.

In the words of Adam Nicolson:

> For Homer of classical Athens was an encyclopaedia of moral choices.[19]

The French philosopher Luc Ferry believes that Greek myths in particular were the precursor to philosophy in that they sought to answer a number of core human questions, such as:

- What is the origin of the world?

- How does humankind fit into it?

- How can you live a good life, avoid hubris (arrogance, overweening pride) and "know thyself"?

- How can you find order in chaos?

- How can you deal with justice and fate?[20]

ON THE TIMELESSNESS OF MYTH:
"NOW THESE THINGS NEVER HAPPENED, BUT ALWAYS ARE"

This was originally written by the 4th-century writer Flavius Sallustius, friend of Emperor Julian the Apostate, in *Concerning the Gods and the Universe*.[21]

In Chapter 4, Sallustius wrote that "myths are things that never happened, but always are." This chapter describes the allegorical nature of mythology and suggests that myths contain – behind their often fairy-tale and fantastical nature – hidden truths and deeper meanings.

Sallustius' observation was cited more recently by Oren Harman, chair of the Graduate Program in Science, Technology and Society at Bar-Ilan University, in his bridge-building book *Evolutions: Fifteen Myths that Explain Our World*.[22]

Harman's book is unlike almost any other work of science, combining an overview of scientific understanding with an attempt to re-enchant science by bringing myth, metaphor and lyricism to the stories of creation and humankind's genesis, while remaining within a robustly scientific tradition.

Sallustius' insight is that myths and stories work because they embody timeless truths about the human condition. As Harman puts it with typical elegance, "myths summon truths beyond our jurisdiction" and are the "expression of existential conundrums, creatures of our lonely searching minds" in that they express deeply embedded human truths.[23]

This should remind us that sometimes stories and myths are the most cogent ways of understanding human behaviour and therefore are the basis for telling emotively memorable stories, creating (brand/corporate) culture and crafting memorably effective presentations and speeches.

ETYMOLOGICAL DIGRESSION

These days the number of books or headlines with 'myth' in them is multitudinous. A quick flick through Google shows *The Myth of Normal*, *The Myth of Race*, *The Myth of the State* and *The BBC: Myth of a Public Service*. I am also quite a fan of Matthew Stewart's *The Management Myth*.[24]

Any book title that manages to combine myth, illusion and delusion is a sure-fire winner: I keep pressing this on my publisher, Martin, who still keeps ignoring my proposal for a book called *The Myth Illusion*.

And there are as many myths being busted these days as ghosts: examples include the BBC's *Trust Me, I'm a Doctor* (2013–), the UK government's Education Hub webpage and the World Health Organization's advice on Covid-19.[25] There is even a science series called *MythBusters* (2003–2016).

Sadly, we now tend to see myth as tainted, imperfect and fake.

But any classicist with time on their hands will tell you that the word *muthos* was itself susceptible to many meanings since as early as Homeric times (around the 9th or 8th century BCE). Myth is almost by definition mutable: there is rarely a single stable and canonical edit of a myth.

Originally meaning anything from 'story' to 'tale' but based on an essential core of truth or historical tradition, it was only later that the polarization took place between the two meanings, with the disparaging sense of 'myth' becoming more commonplace. This should serve as a reminder that we should be careful in dismissing 'mere myths.' In fact, for many ancient cultures, myths not only were the collected tales of heroes but also functioned as society's equivalent of what we've already encountered as TOEs (theories of everything), which attempt to answer deep questions, at least in terms of their own age. Many cultures felt that they were outlining reality in expressing their own worldview on cosmogony (the origin of the universe) or the role of the gods.

Equally, it is often said that the cultures and religions of the East prefer myth and organic, intuitive thinking, whereas the dominant modus operandi in the West is more mechanistic and rational by comparison. But it is also the case that many myths do in fact harden into accepted truth if we fail to pay attention. American journalist and author Bill Bryson notes many famous examples in his ripping book *Made in America*: Columbus, Washington, the 4th of July, cowboys, Ellis Island and chow mein (an American invention) all bear witness to a country striving to self-mythologize in order to both understand and identify itself, at every available opportunity.[26]

FOUNDATION MYTHS

Also known as creation myths, these were traditionally the basis for a city, state, country, religion or tribe to give a sense of purpose, meaning and a beginning. They are tools in various forms – poetry and prose, monumental and decorative art, expressed in civic and religious rituals.

Beginnings – as I have written before in the manifold areas of storytelling – are important. They set the tone, they provide the foundation for what follows and – as discussed in *The Consumer Behaviour Book* – they *frame* what is to come, creating an expectation of understanding.

Many such foundation myths begin with a creation or birth, and some have a supreme deity at their heart. Others place their tribe at the centre of the universe and explain the origin of the universe accordingly (known as cosmogony), with humans (especially the right type of humans) interacting with the gods. Foundation myths do not necessarily centre on a cosmogony.

Rome liked a bit of R&R for its foundation myth.

That is, Romulus and Remus. Their story involved a she-wolf (*lupa*, also being the Latin slang for a prostitute) and a healthy dose of fratricide. Athens' back story was the result of a battle between Poseidon and Athena (clue in the city's name as to who won), and the location of Alexandria came to Alexander the Great in a dream.

Creation myths vary wildly: spiders, serpents and cows feature heavily, and the Dreamtime of Australian Aborigines has earned wider attention. But on the further shores can be found primordial cosmic eggs, the Viking primeval frost giant Ymir, the emergence story of the Hopi Tribe of North America and a decapitated head among the Maya.

According to Douglas Adams's *Hitchhiker's Guide to the Galaxy*, many races believe that the creation of the universe involved some sort of god, though the Jatravartid people of Viltvodle VI believe that the entire universe was in fact sneezed out of the nose of a being known as the Great Green Arkleseizure. It also turns out – spoiler alert – that the earth is in fact a giant supercomputer that was itself created by a supercomputer, called Deep Thought.[27]

H2G2 fans will know that Deep Thought pondered long and hard about the answer to the question of "life, the universe and everything" before finally deciding the answer was … 42.

And we are all familiar with brands that have created their one foundation or creation mythology, and the power that it wields in the collective cultural memory.

BRAND MYTHOLOGIES

VIRGIN BIRTH

Richard Branson is one of the most successful and recognizable business entrepreneurs on the planet: the founder of Virgin created an empire that at its height saw the company selling music, books and games, with a publishing house, a radio station and an airline, and trains intermittently stopping at various UK railway stations.[28]

Branson is a bit more than a one-man brand, and is famed for his self-promotion. But Virgin is rooted in a complex, human and aspirational brand mythology.

At school Branson was hampered by dyslexia, making learning a real torture.

At the age of 15 he realized students didn't really have a collective voice (it was the time of the Vietnam War), so he started a magazine, called *Student*, in which he managed to publish a rather eclectic list of authors, including Jean-Paul Sartre, John Lennon, Mick Jagger and John le Carré. Moreover, he didn't pay the celebrities for publishing their stories.

The next inciting incident (as it's known in storytelling) – serendipity. Young Richard's mother had found a necklace, which she handed in to the local police station. When after three months no one came to claim it, she was told she could keep it. It was worth about £200, which she gave, as what would effectively become seed money, to her enterprising son.

He managed to call advertisers from the phone box, using this money.

As Branson explained:

> There weren't such things as mobile phones in those days. We had a mobile phone box at the school with a fixed line telephone, and if you wanted to make a call, you had to keep putting money into the phone box, and, if I chose the times of day where other kids were not using the phone box, to go and ring up advertisers, potential advertisers, to see if I could persuade them to advertise in my magazine. And there was one occasion where I was putting money in, and I lost the money and like didn't get through, and I rang up the operator, and they said, "oh don't worry, we'll put you through." So then I started using the operator as my secretary. I'd just ring up, say I've lost the money, never put any money in. And so I had these posh operators being put through, "I've got Mr. Branson for you." So I finally had my free telephone calls.[29]

Although the magazine did not ultimately succeed, it gave Branson the financial stability – and confidence – to go and found Virgin Records, the brand name chosen as a reference to his youthful immaturity. And the rest, as they say, is mythology.

THE MYTH OF THE WAFFLE

One of my favourite creation myths is for that niche, small-scale, furtively promoted brand Nike. (Incidentally named after the Greek goddess of victory: you may recognize the Winged Victory of Samothrace, currently at the Louvre in Paris but, subject to negotiations, to be returned to Greece. If you've been to Nice, in the south of France, you witnessed another testimony to the goddess of victory.)[30]

The story starts at breakfast one morning in 1971 (we have a place and situation already in the memory palace of our mind – and incidentally we'll cover memory palaces in *Part Three*), with Nike co-founder Bill Bowerman having breakfast with his wife. The eureka moment occurred when it suddenly dawned on him that the grooves in the waffle iron that she was using might serve as an excellent mould for a running shoe.

Oregon's Hayward Field stadium, where he worked, was transitioning to an artificial surface. According to his wife:

> Bill wanted a sole without spikes that could grip equally well on grass or bark dust.
>
> We were making the waffles that morning and talking about (the track). As one of the waffles came out, he said, "You know, by turning it upside down – where the waffle part would come in contact with the track – I think that might work."
>
> So, he got up from the table and went tearing into his lab and got two cans of whatever it is you pour together to make the urethane, and poured them into the waffle iron.[31]

The rubber mould inspired Nike's first shoe, the Waffle Trainer, which debuted in 1974. The Nike story and mythology deepened from then onward.

(On the subject of sports brands, ASICS has an interesting origin. It is an acronym for "Anima Sana In Corpore Sano," a Latin phrase meaning "a sound mind in a sound body," an adaptation of an aphorism found in Juvenal's 10th satire, written in the 1st century CE. Juvenal also gave us "who will guard the guards themselves" and "bread and circuses," which both have a topical political relevance.)

SENNHEISER: SOUNDS INTERESTING

A few years ago, I was trying to define a foundational story for the Sennheiser audio equipment brand with their then London ad agency. The brief was to devise and project a story internally as an 'internal engagement piece.'

"We need to give those people who sell Sennheiser products around the world a new and exciting story to tell."

The brief was along the following lines:

- Remain true to what the client was already doing, yet add something newish

- Retain – yet develop – their key thoughts: "The Pursuit of Perfect Sound" and "The Science of Sound"

- Dilute the possible risk of 'perfection' + German + cool/cold/clinical tone

- Confront the 'surfeit of truth': facts, and technical and potentially niche details, that might alienate the broader audience

- Choose the right story frame: the Man, the Quest or the Craft? For more on this, see *The Storytelling Book*

The story we alighted on used the actual foundation myth (Fritz Sennheiser in his farmhouse, a lone devotee striving for audiological perfection):

- **Focus on the pursuit, aka the Hero's Test and Quest:** the eternal journey of discovery and self-revelation, overcoming trials and tribulations as part of self-actualization – so, a story that could be both inner- and outer-directed

- **The hero as maverick:** guided by a purpose that is singular, idiosyncratic and non-linear, with an almost Sisyphean reliance on the relentless pursuit of perfection

- **The inner daemon:** the guiding spirit that leads the hero to pursue a path that is pure and fearless of convention

- **Quirkiness:** as with many hero myths, quirkiness operates as an antidote to habituation; great thinkers and scientists often find habit the enemy of progress – the great thinker will appreciate the need to 'think differently'

- **The struggle is the meaning:** as framed by the 17th-century Dutch philosopher Baruch Spinoza, 'conatus' (striving) is the essence of humanity; the quest is the grail, knowledge is the prize, the journey not the destination is the meaning

- **The maximizer's rigour:** for many a hero, perfection is the maximization of possibility – leaving no stone unturned, no assumption unexamined

- **Science specifically is the enemy of certainty:** all science is provisional, and scientists are happiest when confused or faced with a puzzle

DURAVIT: A SANITARY STORY

For those who haven't spent much time looking at sanitary porcelain products or visited many bathroom outlets, let me lift the lid (sorry) on Duravit AG.[32]

Founded in 1817 and headquartered in Hornberg, in the south of Germany in the midst of the Black Forest, Duravit is primarily a manufacturer of porcelain bathroom fittings, though in recent years it has diversified.

Today, it operates at an international level with 11 production plants and a workforce of more than 7,000 employees worldwide.

It has a certain appeal in this context as it has what appears to be a Latin name.

It may originate as a combination of 'durable' and 'vitreous,' but this seems more than an unlikely coincidence. Because Latin scholars (here we go) will immediately recognize the name as the third-person-singular perfect active indicative of the verb *duro*, meaning 'to last' (as also in 'duration' or 'enduring').

Although, if this is deliberate, the company should note that *duravit* means 'it lasted' but in the sense that the thing doesn't exist any more, which is presumably not what they were aiming for.

Yet the brand mythology makes no mention of this, neither does it make much of its links to the Black Forest, which would add to the brand's mythology.

DECK THE HALL

I had the pleasure and privilege of working for a not insignificant period with the Royal Albert Hall (henceforth referred to – as it is affectionately known – as the Hall) in advance of its 150th-anniversary celebration in 2021. It had been founded in 1871 by Queen Victoria and Prince Albert, as one of the core elements of what in London's South Kensington is known as Albertopolis.

In a rather meta way, the story itself has a creation story behind it.

I was speaking at a conference and was narrating a story of my then-young son and the fact that his school had won tickets to see J. K. Rowling read from *The Order of The Phoenix*, the Harry Potter book that she was launching.

There were over 4,000 children there that day. Can you, I wonder, think of a word to describe a venue full of 4,000 excitedly expectant young people?

Yes, maybe 'chaos.'

But then when J. K. R. approached the podium ... silence, expectation, tension.

The point of my story was to demonstrate how we are culturally trained to give storytellers credibility and trust (what Aristotle called ethos) or authority (we will come back to this in *Part Two*).

At the end of my talk, I was approached by someone who introduced herself by telling me that she could verify my story (always good to know, given the vagaries of my ... errrm, what do you call it ... memory), as she was in fact the marketing director of the Hall (as confirmed by lanyard).

The conversation moved swiftly on: "Well, it will be the Hall's 150th anniversary soon, and would you like to help us tell its story to celebrate that landmark?" In an embarrassingly short heartbeat, I agreed, and I went on to help them create a story that was approved and commissioned, only to be – sadly – diluted by COVID-19.

Why did they need a story?

The Hall was unpindownable: the world's busiest venue, a landmark, a tourist attraction and an architectural powerhouse. And a registered charity.

Too often companies and organizations ostentatiously vaunt an anniversary ("Look, we are 100 years old!!! Isn't that amazing!!!!!") to deafening consumer apathy. There was a risk that, on top of the financial profligacy, this would be a wasted opportunity for the Hall to promote, define and express itself.

Of all the challenges, issues and opportunities identified, the one that resonated most across the internal clients was from the original strategy document: how not to squander the opportunity presented by this one-off occasion.

Homework that I asked them to fill in revealed three issues:

- The tone of voice in the Hall's communications was universally described as "fairly informative, positive and professional." So, not exactly emotional, inspiring or warm. And there was a distressing tendency among the Hall's team to use "iconic venue" a lot.

- Most of their communications (and therefore perception) were very event-driven: in the jargon that was bandied about, the Hall was defined as a "receiving house." This seemed awfully passive – as if it was merely a receptacle for the (undoubtedly many and varied) events, gigs and celebrations that it had hosted over its 150 years (there were something like 400 events per year). It had played host to entertainment, education and politics of all types and brows, from populism to profundity, Adele to Ali, Wagner to Winston Churchill, the Krays to Chessboxing. Not just the BBC Proms and the Festival of Remembrance. You can do the math(s).

- To paraphrase one respondent: "We tell stand-alone stories about the history of the Hall (for example, around specific historic events) but there is nothing consistent or pervasive about our history or current brand objectives in our comms."

What was needed was a master narrative that would create coherence, clarity and thereby confidence, rather than see everything devolve into a mass. Although each of the plethora of events had their own audience and agenda, the communications needed to be less disparate.

What we developed to meet those objectives was a character and personality based on three Es: the Hall was defined (emotionally as much as anything) as eclectic, eccentric and electric.

MYTHOLOGICAL CITIES

It's not only stories and brands that can partake of mythological status: many a city, I would argue, enjoys a character that could also qualify as mythological.

Classical Athens went through a form of self-invention after the Persian Wars (5th century BCE), creating the golden age of democracy, drama and philosophy, among many other cultural glories. The contrary myth of Sparta – introverted, militaristic and isolationist – is only a slight simplification.

A brief mytho-cultural-geographical tour would yield:

- The myth of British imperial supremacy and chosenness, buttressed by the arrogation of certain values, such as honesty, decency, moderation and a dose of emotional repression (see Kate Fox's marvellous *Watching the English* – the appearance of another fox[33])

- The myth of American exceptionalism and the American Dream of limitless possibility, universally available

- The myth of Russia as Third Rome, and (in the current presidential aspiration) the restoration of the empire of Greater Russia

- The myth of celestial destiny of China

On and on and on we can go throughout history, identifying stories (myths) being used to justify a nation's or people's existence and actions.

MYTHOLOGICAL FOOTBALL (SOCCER) CLUBS

Or take my love of the English football (soccer, if you must) team Manchester United.

From a North Londoner straddling the geographical divide between the two top North London teams, Arsenal and Spurs, this may need some explanation.

I do have family in Manchester, and when they were young I took my kids to a match at Old Trafford, the legendary home of Manchester United, known as the 'Theatre of Dreams.' This was followed by a holiday in a hotel where the United squad dropped in one day as they were using the training facilities. I thought I would use the opportunity to ask my then five-year-old to speak to "that man over there" and ask him to close the curtains. To this day, my son is the only person in my knowledge to have had the honour of addressing Eric Cantona directly.

But a large part of the reason I cherish United is their mythology: the Busby Babes, the Munich tragedy, George Best, Bobby Charlton, Eric Cantona, David Beckham, Cristiano Ronaldo and Wayne Rooney; the highs of Sir Alex (Ferguson) and the lows that have followed in his wake. The stuff (and Theatre) of dreams, though more nightmare-ish at the moment.

Liverpool is an equally mythic club (and city), but I would argue that Manchester City is not (at least yet). Apologies to my City-supporting cousins.

ADAPTING, CO-OPTING AND REFRAMING MYTHS

So, we look to myths for the timeless and transcendent – prisms through which to see things afresh – and adopt and adapt them in our communications.

In turning to the past, we can reinvigorate and reframe our world to be transformative, liberating and redemptive.

Myths are arguably more prevalent than ever, due in no small part to the ubiquity of social media and the ability to create our own personas and myths (even to act as 'trolls').

Here are some insights – explored further below – that fall out of the section on brand mythologies above:

- Find your brand mythology

- Use story and myth in your presentation

- Use myth in your market research

FIND YOUR BRAND MYTHOLOGY

Look at the brands that you cannot too tongue-adjacently call 'mythical': the likes of Apple, Nike and Virgin; football (soccer) teams like Manchester United or Liverpool; US football teams like the Jets or the Patriots; cities like London, Paris or New York; or London's Royal Albert Hall.

What makes a brand mythology?

Not every start-up or founder can aspire to that sort of creation myth. But if there is even a seed that can be sown, and then mined (mixed metaphor warning!), rediscovered or built on, it can form the basis of a Golden Thread that can be invaluable to the brand, its communication and its agencies.

USE STORY AND MYTH IN YOUR PRESENTATION

Myths usually contain the following ingredients:

- Story and myth trade in **archetypes**. These are certain basic characters (or types) that we find in ancient myths or fairy tales and that continuously recur in world stories, literature, film and art. They represent basic elements in the human condition. A brand built on an archetype can forge a relationship with people that goes beyond the ordinary. Archetypes relate to the deepest emotional and unconscious parts of ourselves that spring from our fundamental universal connection as human beings. They allow expression and understanding of the emotion experienced when engaging with a brand. Think of Virgin as a Trickster, BBC as the Sage or Harley Davidson as the Outlaw.

- There is a **hero** who sees things differently. They may have a passion, a challenge, a destiny or a hobby that needs expanding. And any of these may be rooted in a sense of injustice, of an opportunity not taken, an itch that needs to be scratched.

- There may be an **epiphany** – an insight (see *The Insight Book*) where something is made manifest to the hero and their destiny is foreshadowed.

- In storytelling there is an **inciting incident**: a seminal moment, dawning revelation, or moment of clarity and wisdom where 'everything changes.' Richard Branson in a telephone kiosk taking orders before he even had a company or an office is one memorable example, showcasing his boyish drive, ambition and pragmatism. Or seeing a waffle and imagining a new type of running shoe.

- Story and myth are rooted in **transformation**: often personal but spreading out to the collective or public. Change is at the heart of storytelling. Change is surprise, and, as I am wont to say, if your talk, presentation or brand is not surprising people, what is it doing?

- There is a **villain** – often represented in conceptual form as something that stands in the way of the hero and their ambitions.

- **Character** is key. Again, this is something I have expounded at length, but it is key that brand mythology relies on people: characters that stand for something and that an audience can identify with, relate to and empathize with.

- More simply, a story and myth are things we can **care** about, in a way that mute facts and information can rarely hope for.

- There may be a **connection** to a particular time or place, but one that – as with all good storytelling – can be raised from the particular to the universal. Again, Oregon for Nike, a phone booth in school for Branson, the location and history of the Royal Albert Hall.

- **Memorability** and **communicability** are key, so the story must be susceptible to concise transmission. There must be a core Golden Thread – a memorable image (Branson's phone booth, Nike's waffle iron) that can easily be summoned by a word, a picture or a prop. (Note: props are a hugely underused idea for speeches and presentations. Physical objects can speak in a way that another PowerPoint slide can only dream of.)

For more on this topic see *The Storytelling Book* and *The Storytelling Workbook*.

USE MYTH IN YOUR MARKET RESEARCH

Anyone immersed in the world of business – and specifically market research – knows that there are profound issues with asking people questions about their individual or tribal behaviour.

Perhaps we need to ask people not to remember their behaviour or predict it, but to frame it as a story or myth, as here the real, human truth will be nestled. My personal experience of working in this area is to prompt stories, myths, anecdotes and revelations as a way of wedging open a window into how people really feel about the brand, or the idea that we are investigating.

(Readers of The Consumer Behaviour Book *– and hopefully beyond – will be familiar with this avenue for teasing out what lies beneath the rational self-justifying of System 2 – in Daniel Kahneman's model of thinking – to find the hidden depth and gems of emotional, implicit System 1.[34])*

Equally, those bent on hunting down insights should always seek to find the universal in the particular – what I call UHTs, or universal human truths.

WHY MYTH MATTERS

Thinking about myth and story also lets us see brands for what they are not, what they are opposed to and what they stand in contrast to.

Myth and story work precisely as an antidote to what I have described in *The Storytelling Book* and *The Storytelling Workbook* as the 'arithmocracy': the current (hopefully short-lived) obsession with numbers, metrics and KPIs and the worshipping of them as if they are enough in themselves to affect attitude and behaviour.

Everything we know from behavioural economics (see *The Consumer Behaviour Book*) tells us we need to address System 1, the secret author of our choices and the home of emotional drives that often work implicitly.

So, not only do story and myth work universally at the level of emotions and archetypes, but they are also a perfect reaction against the impulse of the arithmocracy to render everything in the form of dry, clinical facts and figures.

Stories and myths are what we live by.

So, story, as we have seen, can help with the three Cs: clarity, coherence and confidence.

MESSAGING	MYTH AND STORY
1. LOTS OF DISPARATE AND SCATTERED MESSAGES 2. VERY SYSTEM 2 - RATIONAL, NEED COGNITIVE PROCESSING 3. LACKS COHERENCE AND THREAD	1. COHERENT AND CLEAR 2. ROOTED IN UNIVERSALS: MYTHS, EMOTIONS, HEROES 3. BASIS FOR ALL COMMUNICATIONS

A SEGMENTED MYTHOLOGY OF MYTHIC CHARACTERS

Let me introduce one particular application of Greek mythology to your business (brand, communications, culture): part segmentation model, part insight-driver and part presentation booster.

AVOIDING LAZY SEGMENTATION

No, I don't mean a classic segmentation in terms of demographic differentiation: many of those are out of date and notoriously insight-free. These days age and class distinctions are rarely clear or helpful.

If you are going to have a market-based segmentation, at least start with a focus on market or sector behaviour: those who use the brand frequently vs infrequently; those familiar with versus unaware of the brand; those who used to use it but have stopped. (These lapsed users can be an enormous mine of insight: Why did they stop? Was it a deliberate choice, a rejection of something inherent in the brand, such as poor service? Or was it apathy and disengagement?)

All these are, I believe, more useful ways of separating groups in order to prioritize communication (in that each will need distinctive approaches) than relying on largely vacuous descriptions such as 'under 20s' versus '35- to 44-year-olds,' or 'mothers with kids' (no, really).

Two instances that make me fume.

Firstly, the comms industry's obsession with 'millennials,' lumping (clumping?) them together under one lazy umbrella (a great band name in the making), as if they are coherently, homogeneously and coevally identical. I own several children (three, to be precise) and they are all aged within five years of each other. But no one who has ever seen or known them would be naive enough to assume their consensus in anything. It is to some extent a freak of history that they belong to approximately the same age cohort, but that says nothing about what they like, don't like or share in common (apart from a wholesale rejection of what their parents claim to be accumulated wisdom, and a largely understandable envy/resentment of Boomers).

Secondly, I deplore the equally flawed tendency to talk about 'the over-50s.' A cruise client I once worked with described and defined their audience to the agency (us) as 'the over-50s.'

Once I'd stopped emitting fumes, I pointed out that there were people in their user base (I knew – I'd interviewed them) in their 40s who were apathetic, stayed on the ship and enjoyed the 24-hour, non-stop omnivore's buffet. On the other hand, I'd spoken to people in their 70s and 80s who were learning to scuba-dive and took every opportunity to visit all the destinations offered on the cruise, and explore them in every detail.

(For a cup of Earl Grey, I'll tell all.)

BE MORE DIONYSUS
So, why not try a segmentation based on classical characters?

One example adopted by Charles Handy, among others, is based on a slightly simplified approach to the two classical Greek gods Apollo and Dionysus.[35] This characterization reaches at least back to Nietzsche, who formalized a dichotomy between instinct and passion at one end (represented by Dionysians) and order, control and rationality at the other (represented by Apollonians). This idea was also developed in James George Frazer's seminal study of myth, *The Golden Bough*.[36]

The locus classicus (literally) is Euripides' play *The Bacchae*. Produced in about 405 BCE, it is one of the seventeen remaining plays of the great Athenian tragedian (Euripides is said to have composed 100). It was denounced for its wildness and never became part of the classical repertoire. Donna Tartt's 1992 novel *The Secret History* centres on a group of modern-day classics students who try to re-enact *The Bacchae*.

The play is an often violent and lurid exploration of the lethal effects of the active repression of and resistance to our wilder impulses. Pentheus, king of Thebes, opposes the influx of worshippers of Dionysus (also known as Bacchus, aka the Wild One, the Goat-Slayer, the Hunter, the Bringer of Growth and the Reveller) for fear that it will upend the social stability of Thebes, which he is hell-bent on retaining.

This does not end well for Pentheus as – spoiler alert – the followers of Dionysus, the maenads, tear him to pieces and his head is brought on stage by his mother, Agave. The moral of the story, if such it can be called, is to warn of the danger of shutting off or exiling our more animalistic and instinctive urges.

(One of the themes is what would now happily be called gender fluidity: one of the reasons Pentheus is so severely punished is his refusal to accept sexual ambiguity.)

This plays into many of the themes that regular readers will spot throughout my 'oeuvre,' especially in *The Consumer Behaviour Book*.

At the risk of anachronism (mind you, if it was good enough for Nietzsche …), we can picture the distinction as between:

- **Apollonians**: favouring logic and the dispassionate analysis of facts and information

- **Dionysians**: driven by intuition, passion and synthesis

With only a slight change of framing, it is not entirely implausible to recast this as a System 1 versus System 2 clash. And, through this frame, we should be reminded that the rational is not the sum of humanity, and if anything, the Dionysiac, creative, untamed urges must also be acknowledged. Too far for creative briefs and brand positioning? I think not.

Before moving on past the gruesome horrors of *The Bacchae*, we can pause for a quick etymological pit stop.

One of the features of the Bacchic maenads and Dionysians is their belief in ecstasy. These days that word has acquired other associations, but its original meaning is to 'stand outside' – as in, to create distance from yourself in order to find out who you are. See also 'stasis,' as in standing still or pausing.

A second word that can be included in this linguistic pause is 'enthusiasm'. Again, much of the original meaning has been stripped away into something more general and vague, but its original derivation points to being inspired by a god (the Greek word *theos* is still just about discernible).

IT'S COMPLICATED: ODYSSEUS

If you find the Apollonian-Dionysian spectrum too simple, how about we add some more characters to the segmentation?

The hero Odysseus' journey back home after the long slog of the Trojan War (the heart of *The Iliad*) is narrated in *The Odyssey*, from which we get the word ... 'odyssey'.

Odysseus is often described in the Homeric original using the Greek word *polytropos*, a word which features in the opening line of the entire work.

It literally means 'much turned' or 'many turning', and *The Odyssey* is nothing if not a story of a man who turns often on his voyage home. The word is often translated as 'man of many turns' to preserve its literal meaning. Another translator goes for 'having twisty ways,' which nods to the deviousness and deceptiveness of the man (he was the chief architect of the Trojan Horse plot, lest we forget).

Recently, British-American classics professor at the University of Pennsylvania and acclaimed translator Emily Wilson published a new, modern translation, and she translates the word more loosely as 'complicated'.[37] Though not universally approved among the classical elite, this translation has a more contemporary feel in that it plays to

Odysseus' more devious and cunning character: how he uses people on his journey – for instance, his cunning defiance of the Sirens.

My favourite story of his cunning is how he outwits Polyphemus, the Cyclops. After Polyphemus has already killed several of Odysseus' sailors and threatened Odysseus with the same, the hero conceives a plan: his superpower, if you like.

First, he plies the Cyclops with wine. The Cyclops ask Odysseus his name and he replies "Outis" – literally, in Greek, 'nobody.' After Odysseus takes advantage of his drunken state to drive a stake into Polyphemus' eye, the latter screams out to his fellow Cyclopes (note the plural). They ask "Who did it?" To which Polyphemus responds "Outis [nobody] did it," so they assume it is a false alarm. This is clever linguistic play, among other things.

THE MANY MES OF PROTEUS

> I'm a million different people from one day to the next. (Richard Ashcroft of The Verve)

> Strictly speaking, I ought to give a different name to each of the "mes" who would think about Albertine in time; I also ought to give a different name to each of the Albertines who appeared before me, never the same. (Marcel Proust)[38]

Perhaps the Greek god that typifies our age best is Proteus. A son of Poseidon, god of the sea, he was also the keeper of Poseidon's seals. Proteus knew all things past, present and future but was able to change his shape at will to avoid being forced into prophesying.

For, in order to ask Proteus questions, it was first necessary to catch him: trickier than expected, since he was so adept at changing his shape.

When anyone can be anything or anyone they want, the god of shape-shifting* is arguably the truest icon of our age, especially with the contemporary fascination with the narrative possibilities inherent in the multiverse.

(*To be distinguished from Pan, the pastoral god of sheep-shifting.)

WITH A LITTLE HELP FROM HERACLITUS

That we each have a single, unified and consistent self may be a proposition that sounds beyond dispute. But here the twin spheres of neuroscience and postmodernism seem at one in questioning this most basic of assumptions.

The idea that everything, including our 'selves,' may be subject to change is, of course, not new. The notion of eternal change is found as far back as the Greeks. The most notable expression is in the works of Heraclitus, who claimed fire to be the universal principle. This accorded with his belief that dynamism and change were the ways of the world.

He also famously said "panta rei." This may best be translated as "everything flows" or "all is in flux," or even more simply as "things change" (cineastes will recognize this as the name of David Mamet's second movie as director, and fans of Keane will concur that "everybody's changing, and I don't feel the same").

Back to Heraclitus. He also asserted that "you can never bathe in the same river twice."

This is usually taken to have two complementary meanings. In the first, the nature of rivers and matter is such that they are in a constant state of transformation and renewal, so that the river you dip in today cannot be the same as the river you swam in yesterday.

But by the same token, Heraclitus may also be alluding to the principle whereby you are not the same person as you were yesterday. With the benefit of modern scientific discoveries and broader philosophical approaches, we can see this as demonstrating the perpetual flux of our bodies as cells grow, decay and die and our mental lives experience similar vicissitudes.

PROTEAN EGO

Daniel Dennett has written extensively about the concept of the self. It is, he wrote, in need of major surgery. For him, the notion of what he called a "Cartesian theatre" is absurd. Descartes believed in the central role of a mental HQ, which, given the limitations of the time, he sited in the pineal gland, theorizing that it directs consciousness and provides the sense of 'self.'[39]

Dennett preferred what he termed the "multiple drafts model" of self. Instead of a "canonical final draft," with a command-and-control capability, this is more about bottom-up emergence. In this scheme, a stream of stories is perpetually created, subject to revision, addition and relentless editing according to mood or circumstance. Indeed, all forms of mental activity are accomplished in the brain by a variety of parallel processes. At any one point in time, there are multiple drafts of narrative undergoing editing in various parts of the brain (see, for instance, Dennett's elegant, if rather presumptuously titled, *Consciousness Explained*). For Dennett there is nothing more pernicious than the "illusion of the Central Meaner."

This explains why there is such a strong link between the concepts of identity and narrative. Identity is wholly bound up with the notion of authorship, with the 'self' as the centre of narrative gravity. We are the stories we tell (Dennett and others would go further and say stories spin us – we are self-spinners).

Julian Baggini, in his book *The Ego Trick*, explores the nature of the self and concludes that rather than seeing the self as an essence, a solid thing (like a pearl, he imagines), it is truer to see it as a cloud, or a process "perpetually in construction, perpetually contradictory, perpetually open to change."[40]

The idea that gives him his title is that the ego trick creates something that appears to have a strong sense of coherence and singleness from what is actually a messy, fragmented series of experiences, memories and stories – from a brain that lacks a central control centre.

PROTEUS ON FILM

A relatively recent cinematic Proteus is Leonard Zelig. The hero of Woody Allen's 1983 mockumentary named after him, Zelig is a 1920s 'human chameleon' who has no real identity of his own but just wants to fit in. A work that transcends genre, it operates in many of the traditions of the documentary, including 'live' events of the era and interviews with tame thinkers, such as Saul Bellow and Susan Sontag.

But the seamless blending of the fictitious Zelig into real situations and real people of the age not only pre-dated *Forrest Gump* by a decade but also posed difficult questions about truth and objectivity in such documentaries and the demands of conformity.

More than this, *Zelig* is a meditation on identity and reality and reflects other elements of the Allen oeuvre, such as stories like "The Kugelmass Episode" and movies including *The Purple Rose of Cairo* (1985).[41]

In *The Purple Rose of Cairo*, another treatise on reality, fiction and the power of movies to, well, move, the central character, played by Mia Farrow, says: "I just met a wonderful new man. He's fictional but you can't have everything."

A MARKETING/RESEARCH PERSPECTIVE

Many of business and marketing's assumptions about targeting monolithically segmented 'consumers' look *tired* and tested. We are now entering what might be termed the 'Plasticine era' (apologies to palaeoanthropologists), as identity and self are generally less intractable.

But there is still resistance in (at least) one quarter: the notion that there is a unified, consistent, unchanging essence within the mind (heart? breast?) of each consumer. And that, having identified it, we will be able to conquer it and place our brand's flag there before anyone else.

The atomization of identity has become especially central to certain strands of research, notably of the semiotic variety. Virginia Valentine and Wendy Gordon, in their rightly celebrated paper "The 21st-Century Consumer" (a winner of the Market Research Society's Best New Thinking Award), sought to counter what they saw as the over-reliance on simple models of consumer identity and communication.[42] They, too, put great store in the postmodern consumer and what they call the opposition of "mutable and stable identities." The former, they argue, are ever-changing, ambiguous and unpredictable.

So, they prefer to replace the old model of *Person + Act of Purchasing Goods/Services = Consumer* with *Mutable Subject + Communications Mirror = Moment of Identity*. This has the benefit of removing some of the crusty layers attached to the word 'consumer' as well as showing the advantages of a more nuanced understanding of the processes of consumption and communication.

HIGH-FLYING BIRDS?

Let's explore one final selection of myths, united by the ideas of chaos and control, hubris (pride), meriting nemesis (divine vengeance).

The latest book by historian and philosopher Yuval Noah Harari – whose *Sapiens* (2011) and *Homo Deus* (2015) adorn the coffee tables of many of the thinkiest chatterati – is his treatise on and contribution to a subject that could not be more topical and yet timeless – the onset of AI.

In this work, *Nexus*, Harari tells a cautionary tale, warning of humankind's headlong rush to embrace AI without considering fully how it may play into what he sees as our tendency to imagine and summon powers we cannot control. The great storyteller that he is, Harari issues a warning about AI and how humanity must beware creating forces that may escape the limitations of our control.[43]

To make his point, he introduces the topic with recourse to some of the eternal myths, from the classical age and later.

One of the myths he recounts was written by the German polymath Johann Wolfgang von Goethe: "The Sorcerer's Apprentice," a poem written in 1797 but perhaps best known to the world now as the source of one of the magical sequences in Walt Disney's 1940 film *Fantasia*.

The original tale tells the story of a sorcerer who leaves his workshop and entrusts the chore of fetching water to his apprentice. But rather than using the slow and tiring pail method, the apprentice acts as what in marketing would now be called a 'disruptor' and creates an enchanted broom to do the work. At first all goes well, until he realizes that he cannot stop what he has started, and the broom threatens to flood the whole workshop. In anger he breaks it with an axe, only for each part to regenerate into a whole new broom. It takes the sorcerer to return to break the spell and warn against conjuring up what we cannot then put back in the (genie's) bottle. There are earlier examples of this type of story, one being *The Lover of Lies* by the Greek-Syrian satirist Lucian, written around 150 CE.

A SHINING EXAMPLE OF MYTH
But the first fable that Harari spins concerns one of the lesser-known Greek myths telling of humankind's hubris – Phaethon.[44]

Phaethon – the name comes from the Greek word meaning 'shining' – begs his father, Helios, to allow him to drive the chariot of the sun across the heavens for a single day, in order to confirm his divine paternity. Helios agrees reluctantly and Phaethon sets off.

But he soon finds himself unable to control the horses, the sun coming too near the earth and scorching all vegetation and putting the whole world at risk. The king of the gods, Zeus (not actually Jeff Goldblum), is forced to intervene and he sends a thunderbolt at Phaethon, thus restoring order.

IT'S ALIVE WITH MEANING

A similar story that Harari doesn't include is that of Prometheus. Prometheus is one of the archetypal mythic figures of the Greek tradition and shares many parallels with myths from other cultures.

Prometheus (his name means 'forethought') was the Titan god and trickster who deceived Zeus and stole fire back from him so as to return it to mortals. (In the storytelling catalogue this theme is classed as 'elixir theft.') As punishment, Zeus both creates Pandora to punish humankind and administers a singular punishment to Prometheus: he is bound to a stake on Mount Caucasus, where an eagle will feed eternally upon his liver, which will grow again overnight (this scene features regularly in Netflix's *Kaos*).

The myth of Prometheus has been adopted and adapted repeatedly since its origins in classical Greece. In the Middle Ages and the Renaissance, Prometheus' theft of fire and his torment by Zeus' eagle were transformed into an allegory for the human soul seeking enlightenment. The myth has inspired artists, writers, thinkers and scientists as a symbol of technological creativity and inventive genius as well as humanism, reason and heroic resistance against tyranny, as much as a warning against overweening arrogance.

For example, written in 1816 and published in 1818, Mary Wollstonecraft Shelley's *Frankenstein* was strongly shaped by Promethean mythology. In her novel, Shelley conceived of her scientific genius Victor Frankenstein as a Promethean 'fire bringer' for her era. She also drew on what were then exciting scientific and pseudoscientific ideas – the equivalent of fire – about alchemy, chemistry, electricity and human physiology.

In Shelley's story, often hailed as the first modern science fiction novel, we can see a similar story frame of ambition to surpass human limits and aspire to the godlike, with an invariably gloomy outcome. In an article on the tradition of Prometheus, Adrienne Mayor, a historian at Stanford University, puts it like this:

> Like many ancient myths and popular legends about artificial life achieved through mysterious supertechnology, Shelley's horror tale is a meditation on the desire to surpass human limits and the perils of scientific overreaching without full knowledge or understanding of the practical and ethical consequences.[45]

Prometheus lives on in varied forms: as the fifth instalment in the *Alien* movie franchise (2012), a board game invented by a maths teacher from Wiltshire (said to have been played by former UK prime minister Boris Johnson during the pandemic – the game, not the teacher),[46] and something described as "an open-source monitoring system with a dimensional data model."[47]

FLYING HIGH

Our third fable about the dangers of overreaching one's abilities and the catastrophic consequences of unchecked ambition is that of Icarus, who flew too close to the sun.[48]

Icarus was the son of Daedalus, master architect and creator of the labyrinth that caged the Minotaur. The father built two sets of wings of wax, but advised his son not to fly too close to the sun. Icarus, who had grown up in the darkness of the labyrinth, was irresistibly attracted to the sun, ignored his father's advice and fell to his death when the wax melted.

This myth carries a similar moral – but perhaps with an additional angle – that the best advice is worthless if you don't take it, especially if you are a rash young man who reaches too high, leading inevitably to your catastrophic downfall.

BACK IN THE BOTTLE

A similar expression relating to control though not of classical origin is 'the genie is out of the bottle' or 'you can't put the genie back in the bottle.'[49]

The word 'genie' was first used in English in the 1650s to mean a tutelary or guardian spirit. It is derived from the Latin *genius* but, coincidentally, resembles the Arabic word *jinni*, which also means a spirit.

The expression 'the genie is out of the bottle' is derived from Arabian mythology that was introduced to the West with the publication in English at the turn of the 18th century of *One Thousand and One Nights*, a collection of Middle Eastern folk tales.

However, the expression did not become popular until the 1960s, with many speculating that it was the Cold War and the advent of the nuclear bomb that brought it into focus.

(Those of a certain age will also recall watching the US sitcom I Dream of Jeannie *(1965-1970), starring Barbara Eden and a pre-Dallas Larry Hagman.)*

DO THE MYTH

The message of many of these myths or fables is one of chaos and control.

At the heart of them – as well as the heart of many stories from Greek tragedy, the best known probably being that of Oedipus – is hubris.

This is usually translated as 'pride,' but perhaps more meaningfully is something closer to 'overreaching arrogance or ambition' or even 'stubborn recklessness that is punished by the gods with vengeance (nemesis).'

IMPLICATIONS AND INSIGHTS (CUI BONO?)

1. Be more Dionysus – don't rebut and refuse System 1.
   a. It may not end in decapitation, but that's still quite a low bar to set in the communications world.
   b. Perhaps clients might want to look at themselves and ask if they err too much on the side of Apollonians, insisting on fact, rationality and analysis; shouldn't they be more than happy to let their agencies be the prophets of Dionysus, to be the bearers of the irrational and chaotic? Would a rapprochement between both sides be less divisive and ultimately more productive?
   c. How might the relationship between the accountants and the creatives – between producers of briefs and their creative recipients – be enabled by exploring this Apollonian-Dionysian spectrum?

2. Consider using these characters as ways of exploring the different attitudes and behaviours in your market (segmentation). It won't always be an obvious or perfect fit – but, hey, it's got to be better than the standard, and largely futile, demographics (which haven't quite become extinct).

3. Use the characters as metaphors, analogies, or the basis for your story, speech or presentation. If it helps, cast yourself as (and/or imagine your audience as belonging to) one of those segments or characters. Maybe allocate different roles to different team members.
   a. Do you see yourself as Apollo: wise, rational and orderly?

b. Or perhaps you should be cast as the creative muse, spirit of the emotional and instinctive, guide to novelty and unpredictability?
   c. Or maybe Odysseus is your role model: more subtle, devious and cunning? Are you the arch manipulator?

4. Using some of these archetypes in brand development is not new, of course. But, if you are looking for a new way of developing your brand positioning and want to explore an archetype approach, it can be very refreshing.
   a. A storytelling approach means thinking of your brand as one of the key archetypes (see also *The Storytelling Workbook*) and then maybe casting your competitors to see what opportunities for differentiation are available.
   b. Consider which of the gods or heroes we have touched on – such as Achilles, Dionysus, Odysseus or Proteus – could give your brand the edge.
   c. How might that affect your framing, targeting and communications?

5. One other possible application is in trend or zeitgeist analysis. If you fancy a new approach to looking at ages, eras and ways of defining an era (and you and/or your client or audience are tired of talking about 'Gen This or That'), how about framing these ages as 'heroic eras'?
   a. Perhaps start with the Age of Achilles: noble and honest, where dignity, gravity and responsibility were the order of the day.

b. Followed, maybe, by the Age of Odysseus, where life has become more complex and sophisticated and cunning is the new modus operandi.
c. Is this the Age of Proteus and Heraclitus, where the self is malleable and can be moved, stretched and pulled in different directions in different contexts and in response to different stimuli, and never bathes in the same river twice?
d. You don't have to look too far into celebrity or political culture or the arena of social media to nominate Narcissus as arguably the god that symbolizes our age: relentlessly devoted to the self and seeking unceasing validation and adoration from the community.
e. Or maybe, more honestly or depressingly, this is the age of Sisyphus, where we are destined to push the boulder up the hill only for it to roll down with unrelenting monotony.
   i. This is certainly the case for the French absurdist writer-thinkers such as Albert Camus, who were much vexed by the meaninglessness of the universe in a post-Darwinian worldview, with a view of humanity at its starkest. Camus' *The Myth of Sisyphus* ends with "we must imagine Sisyphus happy."[50]
   ii. This is a world where we all feel our lot is to be constantly pushing that boulder up the hill only for it to taunt us with its predictably relentless descent.
   iii. Or perhaps we see Sisyphus as embodying revolt, passion and freedom?

In need of some piquancy and refreshment for your speech?
Need to zhuzh up your pitch or presentation?
Trying to stand out from the crowd, who are drowning in their morass of self-inflicted jargon?

PART **TWO**

VOCABULARY

AUTHORITY

I often start my storytelling workshop by looking at the connection between author and authority. Unless you are a dyed-in-the wool etymologist (we are few and far between) or watch any of the sword-and-sandals TV series like *Those About to Die*, where characters are wont to declaim about 'dignitas' and 'gravitas' in what passes in these dramas for casual conversation, you may be unaware that 'authority' derives from the same etymological root as 'author.'

Without wanting to go too far back into Roman political history, *auctoritas* was wielded by the state and primarily by the Senate (the S in SPQR, Senatus Populusque Romanus: the Senate and the Roman People, an acronym that you can still find throughout modern Rome).

The root is generally thought to be the verb *augere*, meaning 'to increase or grow' (and from which we also get 'augment').

I begin with this history as a reminder of the inherent power of the master storyteller: the ability to captivate an audience (to literally hold them captive, in the palm of your hand) or to encapsulate the myth, history and ethos of a culture or people (think Homer's *Iliad*, Virgil's *Aeneid* or many a religious tome).

And for this we reward them with attention, honour, a TV documentary series or (if they are a comedian) a sitcom.

UK readers may recall one of the more bizarre incidents during the depths of the pandemic, involving a parish councillor for Handforth Parish Council, in Cheshire. One Jackie Weaver, in a now notorious Zoom call that went viral, was accused of having "no authority" to remove councillors from the meeting.[51]

Such was the misery of the Covid era, this passed as entertainment, and she even became a minor celebrity off the back of it.

CHARACTER

While still deep in etymological territory, we can spot some more patterns at work.

The word 'form' entered the modern Western philosophical framework as a translation of Plato's word *eidos*, which he used as the basis for what is called his 'theory of forms' – the notion that there exists a (Platonic) realm where ideal forms exist, and our real-world examples are mere imitations.

This word, which is also the root of the words 'idea' and 'ideal,' came from the Greek word for 'seeing.'

(Eidos is also, incidentally, the name of the company behind the Lara Croft Tomb Raider videogames.)

So again, we can see some patterns emerging: that ideas are shapes or forms, and changing shapeless data into information and information into something more useful requires a shape or an idea with a sense of a guiding vision behind it.

There are connections to be discovered here with the concept of the brand.

The word 'brand,' we sometimes forget, comes from the notion of the branding iron. This was in an era when this was the easiest way to mark and distinguish your cattle from your neighbours.

Two implications arise from this shallow dip into the history of human-bovine relationships.

The first is how inextricably linked the notion of branding is with *burning* something into something else – usually burning the brand name or some associations into people's brains, with all the attendant implications of consumer-as-cattle, and of power, control and ownership (ideas that seem unhelpfully dated to say the least).

The second is the proximity of the idea of 'brand' to that of 'character.'

This latter word – which we see everywhere with meanings ranging from a defining quality or personality to a sense of moral strength to a person with such in a play, novel or movie – has the same root. 'Character' comes from the Greek word meaning 'to stamp, engrave or inscribe.'

So, when brand theorists, such as Stephen King (not that one), then working at the J. Walter Thompson ad agency in the UK, evoked the idea of 'brand personality' in the 1970s, they were on firm historical and linguistic footing, though it was not so much anthropomorphic as bovo-morphic (take that, spellcheck).[52]

When working with brands, I often have to remind clients of the importance of brand character. One of my abiding themes (see *The Storytelling Workbook*) is that we have worshipped so devoutly at the altar of content (what we say) that we have given insufficient attention and love to form (how we say it).

This is where character comes in: no one has to be told that character is essential to storytelling, yet in our communications and websites, we too often put all our effort (and money) into message, facts and information without giving the necessary importance to form, character and story.

ACRONYMOUS FISH

Let's now turn to a famous Greek icon (in all senses of the word). 'Icon' itself comes from the word 'image' or 'picture' from the Greek. An iconoclast literally is someone who breaks or destroys images or idols, and originally referred to mobs who would vandalize religious objects. These days it is more commonly used of someone who tears down established beliefs or principles.

We also see 'icon' in 'emoticon,' a combination of 'emotion' and 'icon.'

In the early Christian era, the fish symbol (sometimes known as the Jesus fish, especially as a popular car bumper sticker in the US) was used as a code that helped Christians to meet at a time of Roman oppression and persecution.

The choice of the fish symbol was based on its strength as an acronym, a compression of a complex idea: the Greek word for fish, *ichthus* (as in ichthyology), was chosen as each of the Greek letters of the word stood for an individual word, creating the sentence 'Jesus Christ, Son of God, Saviour.'

So, a verbal acronym became a visual motif and a secret, shared symbol.

This also ties into something mentioned (albeit briefly) in *The Consumer Behaviour Book* – the concept of heuristics: mental shortcuts, which the brain (unconscious System 1) spots, seizes upon and implements, often without the knowledge or approval of the conscious System 2 process.

Think about how often brands create and own these shortcuts, be they visual (the Apple logo, the Nike swoosh), verbal (a slogan) or a visual mnemonic (the Compare the Market meerkat, the GEICO gecko, the McDonald's golden arches, the London Underground map, etc.).

One equivalent of the ichthus is the acronym.

I am partial to a good acronym, though I do warn of the dangers of drowning in acronym language (DIAL – so maybe 'DIAL' it down?).

(Note: yes, I am aware that to qualify as an acronym a set of letters has to be capable of being pronounced as a word: so Covid and NASA are acronyms, but FBI and BBC are technically known as initialisms. Trying to fend off an avalanche of comments ...)

I tend to feel there is some subjective leeway with acronyms (as with jokes). Some I hate include RGUs (people being inhumanly and dismissively referred to as 'revenue-generating units') and the old railway acronym defining passengers as SLF (self-loading freight).

KING OF ACRONYMS

And I have been known to create or adapt them as simple mnemonics, worth their weight in memory gold.

One anecdote.

I was working in another of the many now-deceased ad agencies I toiled for in a bygone era, and we were pitching for a well-known burger restaurant chain (clue: the other one). To give you some initialism background: the industry referred to itself as having QSRs (quick-service restaurants, or more specifically FFHRs – fast food hamburger restaurants – but the industry preferred the former as it was less tarnished with the 'fast food' descriptor).

We had all the targeting and demographic data we needed, and frankly there was very little that was new to us or the client that we could leverage to create an imaginative new strategy and/or creative direction.

But in what could charitably be called a moment of insight, I thought about recasting the two main target groups in a way that might become just that bit more memorable.

The first group were the heaviest market users, typically aged 18–24 and male (that was about as much psychological acuity as we could apply at the time). The other main segment were parents (male and female) who took their small children for a good-value ('happy') meal, often incentivized by the lure of a small toy.

Nothing to see here.

But, rather than wheeling out the same content in the same form (see above), I coined a couple of acronyms. The heavy user became GEOFF (Great Eater Of Fast Food); the (unisex) parent was dubbed CHRIS (parent of Children with Ravenous Insatiable Stomachs) – that one needed a bit more force-fitting into the acronym corset.

No new content, but the acronyms worked a charm as mnemonics. The client not only recalled them from the pitch but also started using them as shorthands in internal comms and meetings.

So, in some way they may have even contributed to us winning the pitch. (And some years later I bumped into the client, who could still trot out those terms. Ah, the inner reward.)

PUTTING THE META IN METAPHYSICS

Now onto a historical-etymological accident. Those familiar with the term 'metaphysics' will appreciate that it has quite a large word-span and is notoriously tough to pin down (one of the less obvious things it has in common with the Royal Albert Hall).

I will go with this definition from Merriam-Webster:

> A division of philosophy that is concerned with the fundamental nature of reality and being and that includes ontology, cosmology, and often epistemology. ... "It analyzes the generic traits manifested by existences of any kind."[53]

But the word's etymology is quite revealing.

It literally means 'after-physics,' which is often mistakenly interpreted in the sense that metaphysics covers topics that lie beyond the realm of physics and its focus on empirical observation. But 'metaphysics' has a wholly different and far more serendipitously amusing origin.

Metaphysics got its name by a historical accident when Aristotle's book (or 14 technically) on this subject was published.

Aristotle never used or knew the term 'metaphysics,' but his editor (in all scholarly probability one Andronicus of Rhodes) coined it for one very simple pedagogical reason: that he recommends that these books should be read *after* ('meta') Aristotle's works on physics, or more accurately his works on nature and the natural world.

As if Dave Grohl had decided to call his band After-Nirvana.

Incidentally, 'meta' as a prefix also has a modern hipster meaning of its own, occasionally nodding to postmodern self-referentiality and irony. Also, meta-cognitive thinking means thinking about thinking, or thinking about how much money Mark Zuckerberg earns.

THESEUS, MEET THE SUGABABES

We are used to the modern philosopher-kings such as Julian Baggini and Alain de Botton trying their damnedest to bridge the gap between philosophy and life as lived by the rest of us. Try as they can, Zeno's paradoxes or the story of Epimenides, the Cretan who asserted that all Cretans are liars, just don't seem to make much of a dent in TikTok world.[54]

But hark: the fact that the Sugababes philosophically ceased to be the Sugababes only to re-emerge as the Sugababes again unexpectedly brought this arcane conundrum to a broader audience, sending philosophical shockwaves across the entire cultural landscape.

For, with the departure of the final founding member, Keisha Buchanan, in 2011, modern philosophers could bring an arcane philosophy issue to the masses.

Were the replacements who took over from each of the original lineup actually the Sugababes? (This became even more complicated after the three original Sugababes reformed in 2001 under the name of Mutya Keisha Siobhan, before finally regaining the Sugababes name in 2019.)

Still with me?

Others, especially in the business of teaching recalcitrant philosophy students, will now have the opportunity to use their new-found media-savviness to try and Push the Button for their charges. Or even, heaven forfend, Get Sexy.

Many cultures have their own example of this phenomenon highlighting the question of when X ceases to be X: the US has Washington's axe, the French Jeannot's knife (a knife has had its blade changed 15 times and its handle 15 times, but is still the same knife). Then there are John Locke's socks; a possibly apocryphal story where the 17th-century English philosopher proposed a thought experiment where a favourite sock develops a hole. He pondered whether the sock would still be the same after a patch was applied to the hole. If yes, then would it still be the same sock after a second patch had been applied?

The Jewish religion also asks whether the 'grandfather's tallis' (prayer shawl) remains the same if every fringe has been replaced. And science fiction writers have had their own fun speculating on the concept of transporting a person atom by atom, or with the multiverse – for which see, for example, the Apple TV series *Dark Matter* (2024–).

Though personally I really hope that somewhere in the multiverse is a universe where they don't have a multitude of TV series based on the concept of a multiverse.

But if you didn't study Greek Like Me, you may be unaware of what is known in the trade as the Ship of Theseus, a philosophical thought experiment about identity and persistence that provokes questions not dissimilar to those raised by Heraclitus about whether we can ever bathe in the same river twice (as we saw earlier).

The legend was first reported by a Greek-turned-Roman citizen and 1st-century CE biographer and essayist, Plutarch.

Plutarch's birthplace was Chaeronea, about 50 miles east of Delphi and the location of a famous battle in 338 BCE where Philip II of Macedon (with his son Alexander the Great – although ancient sources are silent on whether he called him that: labelling can be harmful to children's self-esteem) defeated the Thebans and Athenians, and in particular wiped out the Sacred Band of Thebes.

This was considered by some to be one of the most important battles of antiquity in that it destroyed the Greek resistance to the Macedonian invader and paved the way for the Macedonians to unite the Greeks for a Persian invasion. A monumental sculpture of a lion, mentioned in antiquity, was discovered in 1818 along with over 250 skeletons, though there is much scholarly debate as to whether they are the remains of the Thebans or the Macedonian dead.

Back to Theseus.

Legend has it that on his way back from Crete after slaying the Minotaur, his ship returned to the harbour of Athens. It was greeted with fanfare and was preserved at least until the lifetime (says Plutarch) of one Demetrius Phalereus, which dates it to around 350–280 BCE (Demetrius was an Athenian politician and member of Aristotle's Peripatetic school, so called because they would wander around as they philosophized).

The point Plutarch was making was that over the intervening aeons, the ship was obviously in need of regular repair, and so as each plank decayed the Athenians replaced it in turn.

The philosophical conundrum here is that after every plank has been replaced and not a single timber of the original ship remains, does it remain essentially the same ship?

This is one of a number of philosophical paradoxes used to explore issues such as essence and identity. What does it mean to 'be' the Sugababes? Can the new band have the same 'identity' (from the Latin meaning 'sameness' or 'same over time') if the constituent parts are completely different? If Keisha, Mutya and Siobhan formed a new band, would they be the true and only Sugababes?

Is this really about structure, shape, relationships, emotion, memory and history?

Is it true that in these cases the criteria for identity fail us? If your experiences change you, and the cellular you is constantly redefining itself, can I say the same About You Now?

Of course, these days with broader issues of intellectual ownership and brand identity, these academic issues are no place for philosophical fainthearts. Some IP lawyers deal with these issues every day and need public discussion of this like a Hole in the Head.

So, maybe we can offer our thanks to the Sugababes – past, present and potential – for legitimizing debate of some troubling thoughts about the persistence of identity.

Or, maybe by now you are getting Overload and just want to Run for Cover.

INFORMATION

As we saw above in the section on character, there is a rich linguistic depth in words that we have too long taken for granted in the world of communications.

So perhaps now a brief stop is required to look at the word 'information' (see also *The Storytelling Book*). As mentioned before, the obsession with content over form has led to some of the worst excesses of communication, from jargon to apathy.

What better way to remind ourselves that information should not be thought of merely as 'stuff' – data, figures, messages and the factual payload aimed solely at conscious, rational System 2 – than by digging into the word 'information'? Without too much excavation, we see the word ... 'form,' a synonym for 'shape.'

So, as I like to say, data is just unformed, inchoate *stuff*. Once we give it shape, it can become information. Everything here turns on the principle of editing and selection – what you take out will give shape, as much as (more than?) what you keep in.

So, we should always be armed with the knowledge that when we say we want to inform, we are seeking to detect, impose and ultimately communicate a form or shape and in doing so forge a relationship with and from our information.

A supplementary concept that is useful here is 'exformation,' coined by the Danish science writer Tor Nørretranders in his book *The User Illusion*.[55] Much of what we take for granted but doesn't need spelling out can best be described as 'exformation' – what we don't need to expressly say or show, because it is taken for granted. I find this concept enormously useful when working with clients on their presentations, speeches and documents. It is a way of indicating what needs to be retained and what needs to be jettisoned in order for their central argument, hypothesis or point to fit what I call the Golden Thread, so it can be as prominent as possible and released from the shackles of the surrounding minutiae.

SYMBOLON:
GOING BALLISTIC

The words 'symbol' and 'symbolic' occur less frequently than they probably should in the world of branding and communications.

Symbol and meaning are not only central to how we live and interpret our lives but also at the heart of a differentiated brand. A symbol acquires its (symbolic) significance through the meaning and emotions it evokes in us. It is a gestalt, something that emerges holistically from different parts (see *The Insight Book* for more on insight as connection).

Its origins lie in the Greek word *symbolon*, with a meaning rooted in 'to throw together.' (We also see the Greek verb *ballein* in ballet, ballistics, embolism and – no exaggeration – hyperbole.)

Another thread that seems to be particularly intriguing ties up loose ends (as it were) from etymology and neuroscience.

The Greek origin of the word 'parable' – a moral story or fable – is *paraballein*, meaning 'to toss or throw one thing alongside another.' The later Latin equivalent is the verb *proiecere*, from which we get the words 'project' and 'projection.'

The neurophysiologist William Calvin has constructed an ingenious theory to explain the sudden explosive growth in the human brain in the past 2.5 million years (the so-called runaway brain). In various works such as *The Cerebral Code* (whose subtitle, *Thinking a Thought in the Mosaics of the Mind*, is worth the admission price alone) and *Lingua ex Machina*, he has outlined a theory of how Darwinian selection could operate in the brain to generate cloning in the cerebral cortex.[56]

But what concerns us here is his ballistic theory (that's a description, not a value judgment).

The essential idea is that throwing – with all its intricate sub-movements and precision of timing – may have been the chief driver behind the evolutionary development of timing circuits in the brain. These, in turn, might have been put to another – and more spectacular – end by the blind process of natural selection. If this capacity for sequencing were transferred to, say, composing music or to uttering or comprehending a sentence, this might provide a great solution to the 'runaway brain' conundrum and provide a bridge for those cognitive scientists and linguists who believe that language was at the heart of our brain's explosive growth.

Richard Dawkins clearly believes in a form of software–hardware co-evolution where the brain is the hardware, and language perhaps the software responsible for pushing the brain into hyper-inflationary growth. In support of this hypothesis, he takes Calvin's observation and asks:

> Could throwing have been the forerunner of foresight itself? When we throw our mind forward in imagination, are we doing something literal as well as metaphorical?[57]

JUMP AROUND

For some the 1992 House of Pain hip-hop track (with *that* squeal) will be evoked immediately, but let's jump around the idea of jumping.

In the pool of communication, where I frequently dip, 'saliency' is a common term, the holy grail of communication: our communication should have cut-through (see the next section), stand out or be top of mind – or be more prominent generally.

Entire areas have been deforested to define saliency and more importantly find ways of delivering it so a brand comes to mind as quickly and readily as possible. Many academic papers have been written on the subject of differentiation and publicity.

But, once again, I just want to focus on the etymology, as 'saliency' comes from the root 'to jump.' Those familiar with the Romance languages will still see and use it in *sauter* (French), *saltare* (Italian), *saltar* (Portuguese and Spanish) and *sari* (Romanian).

('Assail,' 'assault,' 'exult,' 'result,' 'desultory' and even 'sally' and 'somersault' all live under the same linguistic roof.)

Two more links to saliency.[58]

First up is 'saltation.' (You can find more about this in *The Insight Book*.)

Darwin's theory of evolution by natural selection was largely based on what was known as incrementalism: the gradual, linear accumulation of small changes over the long history of the evolutionary record and human change.

A contrasting theory was one of 'saltation,' suggesting sudden, abrupt changes in the fossil record.

Darwin was a gradualist and famously said "natura non facit saltum" (nature doesn't make jumps) in his *On the Origin of Species*.

But in 1972, the term 'punctuated equilibrium' was coined by palaeontologists Stephen Jay Gould and Niles Eldredge to represent the notion that the fossil record does occasionally reveal violent bursts of change, rather than the relentless incrementalism of continuity that most other evolutionary biologists predicted.[59] Though the proposal caused a lively debate among Darwin's heirs (opponents sarcastically labelled it 'evolution by jerks'), it did in part help to explain the lack of continuity in the fossil record as opposed to the gradualist approach, where change would creep along.

(Gould's riposte saw the phrase recast as 'creeps versus jerks': there's that underestimated scientific sense of humour again.)

I am constantly on the lookout for brands, product launches and communication ideas that avoid easy incrementalism or gradualism – aka more of the same – and embrace saltation: taking a leap, or a jump into the unknown.

The second cognate, as they say, is 'consilience.'[60]

Historically, this represented the idea of convergence, the linking together of principles from different disciplines, especially when forming a comprehensive theory, especially in terms of uniting the humanities and sciences.

Historically, consilience had its roots in the ancient Greek concept of an intrinsic orderliness that governs our cosmos (*cosmos* being Greek for 'order').

In the physical sciences, the meaning "elasticity, power of returning to original shape after compression, etc." is attested by 1824.[61]

The word 'resilience' derives from the present participle of the Latin verb *resilire*, meaning 'to jump back,' 'to spring back' or 'to recoil.'

A Google Ngram of the word 'resilience' shows how popular it has become over the past couple of decades, as issues of mental health and wellbeing have come to the fore.[62]

DECIDE:
CUTTING DOWN OUR CHOICES

The Consumer Behaviour Book looked at decision-making through the lens of behavioural economics.

It explored how so much of what we think we are choosing to do rationally, logically and independently is very often nothing of the sort. Because of the brain's biological demand for energy efficiency, it makes a vast array of decisions unconsciously and (as we saw earlier) heuristically, using shortcuts that are frugal (in energy consumption) and fast. This explains why we find many of our decisions are a trade-off between the best and the simplest.

So, one way of looking at 'decide' is to uncover its etymology.

For at its heart is the Latin word *caedere*, meaning 'to cut.' So, 'to decide' sits between cutting away or cutting off: a decision is stripping away alternatives, lopping off the branches from the tree of choice.

Before we move away from *caedere*, here are just a few words that have sprung from the same root: 'scissors,' obviously, but also all the killing *-cides* ('homicide,' 'infanticide,' 'pesticide,' 'insecticide'). Also many medical–dental words (such as 'incisors' and 'caesarean'

– the latter more likely from this root than from Julius Caesar); words focusing on precision, like 'concise' (as in this book); and 'precise.' And, less explicitly, 'cement,' from small broken stones.

A TENTH SITUATION

A short diversion, and one for the linguistic pedants. Ask around and people will tell you that 'decimate' is just another way of saying to reduce by a significant amount, or to kill off in large numbers.[63]

But in the same process of linguistic attrition we see pretty much everywhere (I'm looking at you, 'awesome'), it originally had a more specific and colourful (as in brutal) meaning.

First attested around the 5th century BCE, it referred to a punishment carried out by the Roman army in response to or to prevent a mutiny. In short, one in every ten soldiers in the cohort would be executed by members of his own cohort. The fate was decided according to drawing of straws (literally the short straw).

In the same way, the word 'annihilate' is beginning to part company with its specific meaning – to reduce to nothing (*nihil* in Latin).

In Old English, the same sense persists in the word *tithe*, originally meaning a tenth part of something, then more broadly a tax representing that fraction.

THUMBS UP OR DOWN?

On the subject of TV series about ancient Rome, with *Those About to Die* featuring on Amazon Prime, we witness another common trope – uncertainty about Roman traditions and one gesture in particular.

The expression *pollice verso* is found in the work of the Roman satirist Juvenal. Frustratingly for us it means 'turned thumb,' without definitely saying which way. But debate rages as to what thumbs up and thumbs down originally designated.[64]

Anthony Corbeill, a professor of Latin at the University of Virginia who wrote a book (the book?) on gestures in ancient Rome, argues that:

> Sparing is pressing the thumb to the top of the fist and death is a thumbs-up. In other words, it's the opposite of what we think.[65]

Based on a 19th-century painting by Jean-Léon Gérôme titled *Pollice Verso*, in Ridley Scott's *Gladiator* (2000) Russell Commodus Crowe follows the tradition where thumbs up indicated sparing the life of the defeated gladiator. The same occurs when Emperor Titus is in the same situation in *Those About to Die*.

There is quite a lot of support for the idea that thumbs up actually meant the opposite of the modern convention, and that it signalled the death of the gladiator. In both cases, producers and directors decided to stick with the will of the people (the plebs?) even if it might be historically inaccurate, given that thumbs up now has such a deeply ingrained association with positive vibes.

KOSMOS:
THE FINAL FRONTIER

One of my favourite TV series of the past few years is *For All Mankind* on Apple TV (2019–), a counterfactual drama about the space race where, in an alternative universe, the Russians got to the moon ahead of the Americans. Watching it suggested a small linguistic diversion about how we describe those brave souls who venture into space.

The subject matter – the US–Russia race, its hypothetical counterfactual present and future, and the space agencies in the US (named the Johnson Space Center in this alternative history) and Moscow (Roscosmos) – means there are many references to astronauts. But also cosmonauts.

The Western term comes from Greek *aster* and *naut*, meaning 'star-sailor.' Whereas the Russian equivalent derives from *cosmos*, meaning 'the universe' (so arguably that bit bigger). Some of us remember a TV series from 1980–1981 presented by Carl Sagan called *Cosmos*.

Much of astronomy (literally, 'star-laws') has clear Greek origins. 'Planet' means 'wanderer'; comets were so called as they were seen as having long hair; 'galaxy' comes from 'milk' and 'milky'; and 'zodiac' means '(circle of) small animals.'

But *cosmos* has a whole universe of meaning. Its original sense was 'to order, dispose or arrange,' often in terms of an army (as in tactics and strategy) or a government.

At the same time another strand (as it were) relates to adornment or dressing (usually for women), and especially the art of beautifying the hair. From this – the skill of dress and ornamentation (the Greek *kosmetike tekhne*) – we see the more common modern use of 'cosmetic.'[66]

Another element came to mean order and pattern (as the opposite of chaos), especially in the harmonious arrangement of the universe.

In storytelling, we find a classic theme in the battle between chaos and cosmos, disarray and order (think of any DC or Marvel Cinematic Universe character or film at this point).

NO BUSINESS OF YOURS

Perhaps you are not familiar with the English word 'otiose,' meaning 'useless or futile.' If you are not, I forgive you. It comes from the Latin word *otium*. Any clearer?

Well, you may recognize it by its opposite – *neg-otium*, literally "not leisure" from which we get 'negotiate' and specifically anything businesslike.[67]

The word *otium* has a long and complex history. It is sometimes simplistically translated as 'leisure' or 'idleness,' or even 'boredom,' but it is far more nuanced than that, going beyond simple inactivity and representing rather a time of quiet contemplation and intellectual pleasure. Early on in the Roman Republic, it designated time off from war, but later on, it became associated with an idyllic, Arcadian and rustic context.

Otium was assigned as a time for personal investigation, study, creativity and contemplation – what would now perhaps come under the aegis of personal development.

The Greek equivalent was *schole*, from which an entire stream of words has emerged, not the least of which is 'school' (not something that many of us will associate with leisure or playfulness, let alone contemplation).

In one of his odes, the Roman poet Horace claims that *otium* (peace, contentment, tranquillity) is more important than riches.[68]

To show that this is not some outmoded and irrelevant concept, in 2020-2021 the Guggenheim Museum in New York mounted an exhibition called "Countryside, the Future," and its teaching materials encouraged visitors to look at the concept of wellness through the prism of *otium*.

Curated by Dutch architect Rem Koolhaas, it suggested that modern wellness philosophies and products have commodified the purity of the concept of *otium*.

BE MORE CAESAR

We have already had cause to talk about Julius Caesar and his conquest of Gaul. Let's now rejoin the story and delve into two momentous expressions which arose in 49 BCE.

CROSSING THE RUBICON

The first is now a byword for an irrevocable act that can be life-changing or even world-changing, the sense of 'now there's no going back.'[69]

Some backstory.

In the dying embers of the Roman Republic (from *res publica* – Latin for 'public state' or 'public interest,' though *res* just means 'thing'), a three-man leadership, known as the triumvirate, had been established, composed of Caesar; his great military and political rival, Pompey (Gnaeus Pompeius Magnus); and a middleman, Marcus Crassus, said to be the wealthiest man in Rome at the time.

It was a fragile relationship at best, so when Crassus died in 53 BCE, the Senate turned to Pompey as the only man strong enough to withstand Caesar, who was now in control of vast swathes of land in the north without official Senate support. Caesar used the following period to become the dominant force and one of the most brilliant commanders in military history.

But by 50 BCE, he was ordered to disband his army and return to Rome, where he was banned from running for a second consulship. Caesar's predicament was that he was hugely successful and popular with his troops, and he was obviously reluctant to return to Rome to once again become a humble citizen.

The fateful crossing of the Rubicon occurred on 10 or 11 January 49 BCE. The Rubicon was a shallow river separating Rome from the province of Gaul, where Caesar was still serving as governor. To cross into Roman territory with an army meant starting a civil war, and Caesar was aware that he would be effectively declaring himself an enemy of the state, SPQR.

But if he *didn't* bring his troops back to Italy, he would be forced to relinquish his command and quite possibly give up his military glory, end his political future and even spend the remainder of his life in exile.

(The river, in northeastern Italy, is just south of the town of Cesena. It was known as the Fiumicino until 1933, when academics identified it as the ancient river Rubicon. It was officially renamed in 1991.)

Three days later, Caesar crossed into Italy and seized the city of Arminium (today's Rimini), taking advantage of Pompey's unpreparedness. As Caesar and his forces moved south, Pompey and much of the Senate fled Rome completely. The civil war had begun that would culminate in Caesar's victory and his position as dictator, before his assassination on the Ides of March 44 BCE. That in turn led to more civil wars before Caesar's adopted son, Octavian, defeated Mark Antony to become Rome's first emperor (or imperator), taking the name Augustus.

(The name Augustus was chosen to signify 'majestic' or 'venerable,' a sense still preserved in the adjective 'august.' The month was originally Sextilis – the sixth month – but was renamed to honour the emperor. The Greek equivalent is visible in today's city of Sebastopol in the Crimea, named in honour of its Greek origins – sebastos *being the exact Greek translation of Augustus.)*

The crossing of the Rubicon is one of the most famous historical turning points, a critical juncture in the decline of the Roman Republic and the onset of the Empire.

This is a great source of debate for historians and writers alike (again, in storytelling terms, these stories represent a great source of hypotheses and scenario discussions, aka 'what ifs?').

Was the crossing inevitable? In other words, was the civil war, and then Caesar's assassination, a culmination of forces set in motion long before?

This again links to a theme explored elsewhere, this time in *The Consumer Behaviour Book*: the notion of framing. How do we frame the story of Caesar?

But why have one iconic statement from JC when you can have two?

THE DIE IS CAST

According to the Roman historian Plutarch, writing later, at this critical moment of decision Caesar declared in Greek and in a loud voice, "Let the die be cast!"

Only then did he lead his troops across the river. Plutarch renders the phrase in Latin, for his broader Latin-speaking audience, as "alea iacta est."

PERSONAL ANECDOTE

I remember that when I was first introduced to the expression 'the die is cast,' maybe at age 10 or 11, I had no idea what it meant. 'Die' I knew only as a verb, and 'cast' I associated with actors on TV or films, or with throwing light, voting or something to do with metal. Only after asking awkwardly (now known as Googling) did I discover that a die is simply one of a pair of dice. Therefore, now I tell people to translate the phrase as 'the dice have been thrown.' It's not unlike the roulette croupier's announcement in French: *rien ne va plus* (no more bets, as the wheel is in motion).

In Roman times, gambling games with dice were popular, as was horse-racing (back to *Those About to Die*).

Just as is the case today, once you had cast (or thrown) the dice, your fate was decided.

Before we quit the dice: in art, the principle of the random or 'aleatory' (from *alea*) is well known.

The aleatory was a significant component of the Dada and Surrealist philosophy. More recently, the musician and theorist John Cage was a notable exponent. He used the Chinese *I Ching*, originally conceived as a tool for divination and for making music by chance. For one piece, for example, Cage selected the duration, tempo and dynamics based on the *I Ching*.

The painter Gerhard Richter similarly used random choices, chance and ready-mades (art made from pre-existing objects) to create his first series of Colour Chart paintings. He later introduced chance selection by numbering colours and pulling them out of a hat.

Richter said, "What interests me most about these works is that chance does it better than I can, but I have to prepare the conditions to allow randomness to do its work."[70]

Oh and rather than risk incurring the wrath of Caesar completists, I must mention his three-word summary of his victory in 47 BCE: veni, vidi, vici- "I came, I saw, I conquered."

FINALLY AND UNEXPECTEDLY

The power of Greek or Latin to suddenly re-emerge in the unlikeliest moments or times never ceases to amaze me.

I was reading an article on the *BBC News* website about the spread in Russia of snitching (informing on your neighbours) and a spate of denunciations and arrests as a result. The mood, said the journalist, Steve Rosenberg, was reminiscent of the Stalinesque arrests and purges and had evoked some of the demons of that earlier era.

But what stopped me was this comment on the mood of the moment:

> Russians even have a word for it, one they have borrowed from the Greeks – 'khton.' It means something dark and evil, the monsters deep inside of us.[71]

You may need more than a smattering of Greek to recognize the word chthon, which we see in the not-quite-everyday word 'chthonic' and which means 'from the earth or soil.' It is also associated with the underworld.

If Taiwanese heavy metal is your thing, you will doubtless be au fait with the band of that name and their position as the 'Black Sabbath of Asia.'

A SONG OF BLOOD AND AIR

Apologies to George R. R. Martin, the 'American Tolkien' best known as the creator of the epic fantasy series of novels *A Song of Ice and Fire*, which you might distantly remember as a TV series called *Game of Thrones* (2011–2019), with a TV prequel (*House of the Dragon*, 2022–) into its second season.

I don't want to interrupt him or his lawyers, as I know his readers are feverishly awaiting the sixth book, as long (1,500 pages allegedly) as it has been long delayed.

But my own story of blood and air, though less epic, was dramatic in its own way. It was maybe not quite as gory as the world of Jon Snow and the White Walkers, but nervous readers may still want to sit down with their alcoholic beverage of choice for a moment.

And though it was not exactly a Greek tragedy, it did – spoiler alert – have a classical Greek tinge, hence its relevance here.

So, in October 2022, I was having a short break away with my wife when I took a shower after she had just taken a bath (relevance: there were bubbles from the bubble bath still in the stand-up shower). One slip on the bubbles, and next thing I know I fall, banging my ribs forcefully on the side of the bath. It became painfully clear that something painfully significant had happened, as I couldn't actually breathe.

After a minor eternity, I was taken to a hospital in the middle of England, where I was diagnosed with a hemopneumothorax (though I wanted to retain the extra 'a' – haemopneumothorax – as in the UK we generally prefer to keep our diphthongs intact; see also diarrhoea, as it were).

Haemopneumothorax, I swiftly learned, is a combination of two medical conditions, both affecting the lungs: pneumothorax and haemothorax. Pneumothorax, which is also known as a collapsed lung, happens when there is air outside the lung in the space between the lung and the chest cavity (often known as the pleural space).

A haemothorax is defined as when there is blood in the same space. Only about 5%, it is said, of patients with pneumothorax experience haemothorax at the same time. Reader, I was that 5%.

One medical website lists possible causes this way:

> Examples of a trauma or injury that could cause hemopneumothorax include: stab wound, gunshot wound, puncture from a broken rib [and others].[72]

Given the reference to gunshot wounds (not to mention the spelling), it is safe to say it is probably a US-based website, as collapsed ribs from gunshots are, I suspect, rather rarer in rural Warwickshire.

But what an etymological treasure trove.

Firstly, *haemo-* comes from the root of 'blood' (as in 'haematology').

Secondly, the *-pneumo-* part is familiar from many words in the English language, such as 'pneumatic,' covering various systems relating to air, air pressure and drills (it's also a more coarse slang description). More broadly, the word is related to 'breath.'

(The French more commonly know the word pneu, *meaning a car tyre, where the initial 'p' is sounded.)*

And thirdly, anyone who has the lightest acquaintance with Greek military history (the Trojan, Persian or Peloponnesian Wars, or the campaigns of Alexander the Great) will be wholly familiar with the Greek word *thorax*, originally denoting a breastplate or cuirass. Now, its meaning has expanded to mean 'chest' in medical circles.

Now let's look at the word 'pleural,' which comes from the Greek word meaning 'side' or 'ribs.' The singular is *pleuron*, and so the plural of *pleuron* is *pleura*.

And finally, any book about advertising and marketing would not be complete with a reference to aspiration. (I am often wont to pontificate that advertising is 80% perspiration and 20% aspiration.)

But in this case (again – squeamishness warning) aspiration refers to a hollow needle with a small flexible tube (catheter) that is inserted between the ribs into the air-filled space that is pressing on the collapsed lung.

Once again, 'aspiration' has a common root – meaning 'to breathe,' from *spirare*, and also plainly evident in words such as 'spirit' as well as 'conspire,' 'expire' and 'inspire.'

Oh, and act three?

The aspiration didn't successfully drain the pleural liquid (it remained singularly stubborn), so I had to attend a second A&E, where I spent four days with an intercostal chest tube inserted (from *costa* – pertaining to the ribs).

CUI BONO: INSIGHTS

1. Never underestimate the importance of authority: remember the wise words of Gerald Cartman (for *South Park* fans) – as an author, you have authority.
    a. Telling a story, weaving a thread, finding the right anecdote or *le mot juste* – all these will enhance your authority with your target audiences and/or stakeholders.

   b. As Aristotle reminded us, two of the three elements of persuasion are *logos* (fact, information) and *pathos* (feeling, emotion). Those we are probably familiar with. But his third leg – *ethos*, the sense of credibility and authority – is as vital as the others, and good storytellers, presenters, speakers, politicians and (dare I say) stand-up comedians know the importance of mastering this quality.

2. Understand brands as acronyms or heuristics.
   a. Abbreviating a message to make it simpler for the brain to process and to create a tribe of meaning (as I like to define a brand) is as old as the Christians in Rome devising the fish logo as a cult totem.
   b. Creatives know the value of a pithy slogan, an unforgettable logo, or a word to define a brand or its mission (the UK's Channel 4 and 'mischief' remain a personal favourite).

Or look at the universal and timeless power of the acronym SPQR (which, as we've seen, in Latin stood for 'the Senate and the Roman People' and represented the twin pillars of Roman democracy).

It is still to be seen throughout Rome on the city's coat of arms, wherever good inscriptions can be found (for example, on the Arch of Titus) and even on the city's drain covers (see picture). What a memorable heuristic it is (even though many people may be unaware of its specific meaning: its place as the fundamental mark of the Eternal City, a mark of its glorious history).

It is such a fundamental part of Roman and Italian culture that – as with any symbol – it has been subverted, reinvented and satirized.

Two instances.

In 2010 the leader of the Northern League political party, Umberto Bossi, either insulted the proud Romans or made a joke (as he claimed later, trying to self-correct) when he said SPQR stood for Sono Porci Questi Romani ('they're pigs, these Romans').[73]

An earlier and more jovial reinterpretation comes from the *Astérix and Obélix* comic books. Obélix often calls the Romans crazy: in the original French, "Ils sont fous ces romains" (literally, "They're crazy, these Romans"). But in the Italian editions, this is translated as "Sono pazzi questi Romani," abbreviated as SPQR.

c. But across all our communications (speeches, presentations, pitches and documents), we should

all make use of these mnemonic devices: soundbites, acronyms, concise expressions.
   d. But beware of allowing yourself to be engulfed in a tsunami of acronyms, especially those that are designed to be cold, clinical and inhuman.
   e. And remember the first of our jumping words – will it be salient and jump out?

3. Be iconoclastic.
   a. Too many brands and services – too much of the communications we pump out – are homogeneously inert and generically lifeless. They fail to get through what I now call 'attention spam.'
   b. Whether in workshops, awaydays or blue-sky thinking opportunities, we must take time out to do some counterfactual scenario planning and imagine the impact if we 'smash our idols.'
   c. If we want to safeguard against actual or potential competitors, or just want or need to refresh or reset our brand, why not smash that icon or remake that image?
   d. One way of casting this would be as a Jump Around session. Deliberately pose yourself (or get your agency to pose) questions to examine whether you are being too gradualist or incrementalist in your market and/or communications. Could someone come in and challenge you with the next saltation, or can you get ahead of them?
   e. How about naming this a disruptive saltation session?

4. Make use of the aleatory.
    a. Let the die be cast.
    b. Like those schools of art where the random and chance led to spurts of creativity, apply what is sometimes known as 'combinatorial playfulness' to promote insight and imagination in a world where collage, montage and bricolage, riffs, cover versions, reimaginings, reboots, sampling and palimpsests are evident across so many art forms.

5. Use the idea of cosmos versus chaos.
    a. This is an idea (just between us) that I use a lot in storytelling workshops, when I am helping clients to tell a story by engineering a conflict as the basis for their Golden Thread (for more on this, see *The Storytelling Workbook*).
    b. One of the great timeless storylines or threads is the opposition of chaos and control. So, how can you put this into practice in your next sales presentation, research debrief or speech to the sales force?

6. Remember the importance of *otium* in our lives.
    a. The separation of *otium* and *neg-otium* can still ring true (especially in our hyper-connected, always-on existence).
    b. One aspect in particular – which I have touched on elsewhere (in *The Insight Book*) – deserves emphasis. To my mind, *otium* allows us – and the brain – time to incubate.

c. *Neg-otium* is when the brain is in business mode, if you like, where efficiency and productivity are the order of the day. To be more creative, to allow the conditions for insight to be brewed, we need to allow – perhaps even to institutionalize – *otium* at the individual, corporate and societal levels.

7. And, finally, always keep one eye on the Sugababes.

Join me in my campaign to ban acronyms – No More Acronyms #NMA.

> **The duty and office of rhetoric is to apply reason to the imagination for the better moving of the will.**

Francis Bacon

PART **THREE**

PERSUASION

RHETORICALLY SPEAKING

Why rhetoric, you ask? (Is this a rhetorical question?)

Because it may have a classical origin – along with philosophy, science and democracy – but as with those pursuits it remains core to the human condition – in its more modern guise of persuasion, influence or communication.

I would argue that one of the key requirements not only of business leadership, an education system or political influence but also of a functioning democracy is the role of reasoned persuasion: hence rhetoric. Despite the censure and critiques often directed at rhetoric (so often prefaced by 'mere'), I firmly side with Tony Blair's former speechwriter, Philip Collins, in arguing that rhetoric is key to sustain a thriving (and functioning) democracy.[74] The fact that rhetoric emerged at roughly the same time and place as persuasion (6th or 5th century BCE in Athens) shows us how tightly they have been – and remain – interwoven.

This is a topic I have come back to again and again as it is rooted in two of my favourite topics: storytelling and persuasion. I have often said that I would ideally call my training sessions and talks 'rhetoric' but then no one would come – so, storytelling it is.

But I think we can go back to Greece and Rome and learn so much about the art of communication and persuasion: how to compose and deliver effective speeches, land persuasive arguments and create tedium-free presentations.

Gorgias of Leontini, the great 5th- and 4th-century BCE sophist philosopher and master of rhetoric, said:

> Speech is a powerful lord that with the smallest and most invisible body accomplished most godlike works. It can banish fear and remove grief, and instil pleasure and enhance pity. Divine sweetness transmitted through words is inductive of pleasure and reductive of pain.[75]

Rhetoric, according to Aristotle, was "the ability, in any given cast, to discern the available means of persuasion."[76] The basic job of a rhetorician is to discover the best available means of persuasion.

And the importance of rhetoric in the first age of enlightenment that was Athens in the 5th century BCE can be seen in two texts. Firstly, in 423 BCE comic satirist Aristophanes wrote *The Clouds*, in which he mercilessly (and joyously) satirized Socrates by making him persuade a boy that it is right to beat up his parents. The parents return later to seek vengeance and burn down Socrates' "thinking shop."[77]

Later on, Francis Bacon wrote:

> The duty and office of rhetoric is to apply reason to the imagination for the better moving of the will.[78]

This was Bacon's way of arguing that rhetoric was about the control and translation of emotion into language that would be both palatable and convincing to a given audience. Bacon insisted that reason "is disturbed" by the emotions: our emotions should not be suppressed, he believed, but neither they should not be in control.

THE ORIGINS OF RHETORIC:
3 + 4 = 7

Where did rhetoric originate, and why did it become so important in educational circles, especially in the UK public school system?

The traditional division of the liberal arts into seven implies an internal division in two branches, called respectively the trivium and quadrivium: the way of three and the way of four.

This division goes back to the classical Greece of 500 BCE and became a source of wisdom and intellectual enlargement for the 'liberal man' (sic) that was codified in education and religion during the Middle Ages.

The seven liberal arts were bound together by a philosophical approach to discovering the first principles of the universe and humankind.

(Etymologically speaking, 'trivium' means a place where three roads meet. The meaning of 'trifling' seems to have emerged as late as the early 20th century via the sense of three roads meeting in an open, public or common space, which later evolved into the sense 'insignificant.' Many of you will hopefully recall the board game Trivial Pursuit, which was (little-known fact) launched in 1981.[79])

The philosopher Boethius (c. 477–524 CE) devised a curriculum, following on from a tradition that went back to Plato, that divided the seven liberal arts into a more elementary linguistic trivium (grammar, rhetoric and logic) and a more advanced, mathematical quadrivium (arithmetic, astronomy, geometry and music).

In about the 1130s, Hugh of St. Victor said, "grammar is the knowledge of how to speak without error; dialectic is the clear-sighted argument which separates the true from the false; rhetoric is the discipline of persuading to every suitable thing."[80]

Sister Miriam Joseph, in *The Trivium: The Liberal Arts of Logic, Grammar, and Rhetoric* (2002), described the trivium as follows:

> Grammar is the art of inventing symbols and combining them to express thought; logic is the art of thinking; and rhetoric is the art of communicating thought from one mind to another, the adaptation of language to circumstance.[81]

ETHICS AND PERSUASION

But scratch beneath the surface of rhetoric, past influence and persuasion, and for some the lowest stratum is bombastic manipulation.

We can look at John Locke's withering indictment in his *An Essay Concerning Human Understanding* (1690):

> All the artificial and figurative application of words eloquence [rhetoric] hath invented, are for nothing else but to insinuate wrong ideas, move the passions, and thereby mislead the judgment.

Locke also described rhetoric as "that powerful instrument of error and deceit."[82]

The American poet Ezra Pound echoed Locke in an article in 1914:

> Rhetoric is the art of dressing up some unimportant matter so as to fool the audience for the time being.[83]

Now let me be upfront. As someone who cut their teeth (and dentures) in advertising, I am not going to ascend the moral high ground. I have done my fair share of saying no to brands or causes that I refused to work on (cigarettes, certain political parties). But as with the law one can argue that as long as it isn't immoral or illegal, it can be promoted.

However, there has always been, back to the time of Gorgias, an awareness of the power of persuasion to manipulate us seemingly against our will. One of the more recent manifestations has been the arrival of behavioural economics as a popular and seemingly effective form of persuasion (see *The Consumer Behaviour Book*).

There are a number of semantic fronts in this truth-storm.

Nothing more needs to be said about 'fake news,' disinformation and what comedian Stephen Colbert termed "truthiness" in a segment on *The Colbert Report* in 2005:

> It's the quality of knowing something in your gut, or your heart, as opposed to in your head. I don't trust books. They're all facts, no heart.[84]

Some neuroscientists and cognitive scientists would call this 'motivated reasoning.'

I'M SPINNING AROUND
(APOLOGIES TO KYLIE)

'Spin' has become the favoured pejorative term for describing information you don't like or agree with.

As well as sharing their name with a pretty much one-hit-wonder ("Two Princes") band, spin doctors have earned a reputation – especially in the world of politics, PR and news management – of being the sort of devious Machiavellians who unscrupulously mould and manipulate the truth in order to serve their masters.

As a term, 'spin doctor' took off in the 1980s, especially around the televised US presidential debate of 21 October 1984, between Ronald Reagan and Walter Mondale. In the UK much of this concept was first pinned on Tony Blair's press secretary, Alastair Campbell. The two were ruthlessly satirized in the likes of TV series such as Armando Iannucci's *The Thick of It* (2005–2012), with the creatively foul-mouthed Malcolm Tucker.

Let's pause for a moment to unpick the meaning. For 'spin,' there are considered to be two plausible derivations.

The first is from the realm of sport, where it refers to the spin that is used in the likes of cricket, snooker and tennis (topspin, sidespin, backspin, etc.), in which a ball is deviated from its natural course. So, people who practise spin are giving a slant to their information or story.

The other (figurative) origin is one that I have much time for, as regular readers will know. It suggests a link with what I have frequently referred to as the Golden Thread, from the story of Theseus and the Minotaur. This is a common metaphor in so many ways: from spinning a yarn to fabricating a story all the way to the hidden etymology in the word 'text' (as in 'textile' or 'texture').

The 'doctor' component refers to the sense of tampering, as in 'doctoring a photo' or 'doctoring the results.'[85]

There are various techniques that are typically deployed by doctors of spin (maybe better called PhDs), many of which have become increasingly transparent because of the internet's ability to spot, analyse and 'correct' them in almost real time.

They include presenting facts selectively (so-called cherry picking), burying bad news (ensuring something that your 'side' considers awkward or embarrassing is only issued when attention is focused elsewhere) and 'sexing things up.'

One of my favourite expressions, discussed in my book *The Inspiratorium*, is 'mistakes were made.' One test to indicate the influence of spin (medically induced or not) is to look for this wondrous weasel phrase. Traditionally used by people in power when in Shaggy mode ("It Wasn't Me"), it is an elegant use of what is known in grammatical circles as the 'exculpatory passive.' In other words, it's an apology (there were mistakes) that isn't actually an apology (translation: I didn't actually make them, someone else did, it's their fault, leave me alone, go and complain to them).

IT'S BENIGN O'CLOCK

Another front that has opened up in recent years features the authors of *Nudge*: Richard Thaler and Cass Sunstein. Given their interest in the use of government and public sector communications to change behaviour, they deploy an interesting phrase: "benign paternalism." You don't have to be George Orwell to note the tension in this expression.[86]

Firstly, there's the semiotics of 'benign' (which almost always brings to mind its opposite – 'malignant'). But then, juxtaposed with 'paternalism,' with its echoes of patronizing, class-based hierarchy, it hardly feels reassuring.

And of course, one person's benign paternalism is another's autocratic tyranny.

But perhaps some judicious prudence needs to be applied. Any form of persuasion needs to be seen in the light of the ability of good communication to affect our actions: whether it's spinning, framing or fabricating (that thread metaphor won't release us), we are always in some way or other, consciously or unwittingly, to a particular end or harmlessly, giving an interpretation of 'the facts.'

So, why exactly is the brain a pretty good scientist but an even better lawyer seeking arguments and justifications? The brain seems to start with a conclusion, find a story and then only later seek evidence to confirm it. Which brings us to ...

LAWYERING UP

One discipline that relies on the power of persuasion is the law.

So, let's look at the CBS TV series *The Good Fight* (2017–2020). A spin-off of the successful legal drama *The Good Wife* (2009–2016), it follows some of the characters from the earlier series, notably Diane Lockhart (played by Christine Baranski) and Maia Rindell (*Game of Thrones*'s Rose Leslie), as they join a prestigious African-American law firm.

But it is Michael Sheen's character, Roland Blum, an impish, mesmerizing and scene-stealing attorney influenced by notorious US attorney Roy Cohn, whom we want to focus on here.

In Season Three, Episode Two, we witness the following exchange:

> Michael Sheen: As attorneys, we are not finders of fact. We are tellers of story.
>
> Rose Leslie: We take the evidence and we craft it into a coherent narrative. We base the story on the evidence, no?

Michael Sheen: No, we base the evidence on the story. Whoever tells the best story goes home with cash and prizes.

[Later] Stories beat facts ... every time.

As for lawyers, so for anyone engaged in any act of persuasion.

A LITTLE SOPHISTICATION

But for Plato rhetoric was not an unmitigated good: he labelled it "the art of enchanting the soul."[87] Plato saw those like Gorgias who taught rhetoric as teaching the skills of lying in return for money, and therefore as a great danger to a civilized society.

Sophists in the Greece of the 5th century BCE were a new type of intellectual – professional educators who toured the Greek world offering instruction in a wide range of subjects, with a particular emphasis on skill in public speaking and the successful conduct of life.

Take the modern definition of the word 'sophist.' As well as the narrow label of Greek speakers around the time of Plato, its broader meaning (here from Merriam-Webster's dictionary) is "a captious or fallacious reasoner," while the Cambridge Dictionary is equally damning:

> A person who uses sophistry (= clever but untrue arguments) in order to deceive people.[88]

Ouch.

Plato's views on rhetoric were in contrast to the sophists, who were skilled in persuasive speaking and often taught rhetoric as a valuable skill for success in politics and public speaking. Plato covers this topic in many of his works: in *The Apology* (which in its original Greek sense means more like a defence than the current usage), Plato shows us how Socrates was put to death in part because he was suspected of being a sophist, a clever rhetorician who twists words and makes the weaker argument into the stronger and teaches others to do the same.

The sense originates in *sophos*, meaning 'wise,' 'clever' or 'shrewd' (the noun Sophia has become a popular name, and we see it in the Hagia Sophia, one of the names of the Grand Mosque in Istanbul), so *philosophos* means 'lover of wisdom.' The sophists were so called because they handed out advice on persuasion, but later this became tainted because of the 'making the weaker argument stronger' allegation and they became (as we see in Plato) a source of contempt and caricatures of the worse form of demagoguery.

(The words 'sophisticated' and 'sophistication' have had quite the etymological journey. They originally had the sense of 'adulterated,' and only seem to have achieved the modern meaning of "worldly wisdom, refinement, discrimination" in English around 1850.[89])

CICERO AND THE FIVE CANONS

> Now nothing in oratory is more important than to win for the orator the favour of his public, and to have the latter so affected as to be swayed by something resembling a mental impulse or emotion, rather than by judgment or deliberation. For men decide far more problems by hate, or love, or lust, or rage, or sorrow, or joy, or hope, or fear, or illusion, or some other inward emotion, than by reality, or authority or any legal standard, or judicial precedent, or statute. (Cicero, *De Oratore*[90])

As well as being a major statesman, the West's first and most illustrious lawyer, and central to the politics of the late Roman Republic, Marcus Tullius Cicero was a scholar and thinker.[91]

Any student of the decline of the Republic will understand Cicero's centrality to that era and know of his own tragic story.

In 45 BCE, he found himself at what was perhaps the low point of his life. Having participated in the civil war between Caesar and Pompey on the losing side, he found himself living powerless under Caesar's dictatorship, with the Republic all but in ruins and many of his friends in exile. He had endured a messy divorce and an equally messy brief remarriage, and, worst of all, his beloved daughter Tullia had died in childbirth.

Part of his writing spree – we have 52 of the 80 legal speeches he gave, and over 900 letters he wrote to family and friends – was devoted to philosophy: through his writings, precious knowledge has been preserved about the Epicurean and Stoic schools, whose original works have largely been lost.

But rhetoric was an obsession for him and the corpus of his writings on the subject spanned his whole life: it is quite possible that he needed to master the art of persuasion in order to pursue his political career. As a *novus homo* ('new man'; we would probably say 'member of the middle class'), he lacked the aristocratic connections that would have enabled him to move up the political ladder, so instead he became a master of legal speeches.

MAGIC NUMBER THREE

We can do worse than summarize Cicero's goals with his own three-word mantra: he phrases the aim of the orator as "docere, delectare et movere": to prove, to delight and to move (that is, to move emotionally, as 'motion' is still the main etymological root of emotion).[92]

According to Cicero, the proving (or teaching) should appeal to the intellect of the hearer by means of logic; the delight is afforded by a euphonious style, and by fables and stories; while finally, the audience is moved to action by the appeal to their feelings.

Part Two outlined Aristotle's three elements of persuasion – *ethos* (credibility and authority), *logos* (facts and information), and *pathos* (appeals to feelings or emotions) – and Cicero gives his own take.

CANON FODDER

Next let's look at the five canons (or tenets, or stages) of rhetoric that Cicero explored across various of his writings.[93]

Even now they can enlighten seekers after rhetoric with clear guidance in crafting a speech, essay, document, lecture, presentation or other work of persuasion, so that it appeals to the intended audience and persuades them (at least in Cicero's original goal) toward ideals such as truth, goodness and beauty.

Let's look at each in turn and explore what the goal and guiding question are for each canon.[94]

INVENTIO (DISCOVERY)

Inventio is not quite the same as our word 'invention'; it is more accurately translated as 'finding' or 'discovery'. This is no mere semantic quibble for philosophers of ontology and epistemology: do we 'find' the word (as it is) or do we invent it?

So, this first phase represents discovering the most effective means of persuasion (again going back to Aristotle). In that sense, it is the most crucial part of any speech or piece of writing, as it is about finding the right topic (as the ancients called it, from the word *topos*, meaning 'place', as in 'topography') from which to build the basis of your argument or hypothesis: get that wrong and the rest is irrelevant.

During this preliminary phase, it is essential that you don't skimp on timing, so finding your topic (aka Golden Thread) is worth every moment spent on it.

I have written extensively on the Golden Thread, but as a brief reminder, it should:

- Be clear, concise, coherent and idea-led

- Be tight as a thread, so your audience do not (literally) lose the thread

- Be a hypothesis, point of view or argument

- Act as what Philip Pullman called the "path through the woods" or, as screenwriter and director David Mamet said, the equivalent of "where do I point the camera?"[95]

- And (does it need saying?) must obviously be based on an understanding of your (target) audience and their needs, expectations and issues.

Goal: To find your Golden Thread, key topic, hypothesis or argument.

Key question: What is the most powerful, relevant and meaningful idea I can convey, and what emotion do I want to evoke in my audience?

Action: Ponder and/or brainstorm ideas, and plan and evaluate different threads. Storyboard them (as many as you think are plausible) and explore them with colleagues.

DISPOSITIO (ARRANGEMENT)

This concept is also known in Greek as *taxis*, from which we get 'tactics' – the way the general arranges their troops to meet the enemy, one of the various military terms subsumed into marketing (see also 'strategy,' 'campaign,' 'target,' 'slogan,' etc.).

It is quite straightforward, following on from *inventio* and your Golden Thread. Once you have established and agreed your thread, the next task is to devise the system or scheme for arranging your material in the optimal manner to achieve your objectives and the maximum amount of persuasion.

The classical rhetoricians, such as Cicero and Quintilian, broke this stage down further into (generally) six parts:[96]

1. Introduction (*exordium*):
   - The opening. This is hugely important in setting the tone, introducing the *ethos* (authority, credibility) of the speaker or making their case. But also, as I have covered elsewhere (see *The Storytelling Book*), beginnings are core to any form of communication in that they set the scene and frame what is to come.
   - Journalists call it the 'lead' ('lede' in journalism jargon).

> "An *exordium* is a passage which brings the mind of the auditor [listener] **into a proper condition to receive the rest of the speech.**"[97]

2. Statement of facts (*narratio*):
   - A description, exposition or summary of the argument that follows. The salient features or facts that are core to the Golden Thread.
   - Cicero characterizes the *narratio* as "gentle persuasiveness and insinuation" while Quintilian says it should be "lucid, brief and plausible."[98]

> "In a piece of deliberative rhetoric, *narratio* is only supposed to include the facts that are germane to the presentation the speaker wants to make to their audience, **not saying more than the case demands**."[99]

3. Division (*partitio*):
   - This divisioning or partitioning is a roadmap for the claims to come, the goal being to name and list the key issues to follow.
   - This is where the speaker lays out not just what they think, but why it is they think that.

4. Proof (*confirmatio*):
   - As you'd expect, this is the section where proof is given, and the speaker will expound positive proofs to strengthen their argument with the supporting material that they hope will convince their audience.

5. Refutation (*refutatio*):
    - The *refutatio* provides negative proofs, acknowledging that other opinions do exist and may have merit, while also demonstrating why those claims do not warrant rejection of the argument.
    - It is far better for speakers to attempt to refute their opponent's or audience's objections in advance than fail to anticipate objections to the argument, or worse still ignore them completely.

6. Conclusion (*peroratio*):
    - I discussed the importance of endings in *The Storytelling Book* and *The Storytelling Workbook*, outlining the scientific evidence of Barbara Fredrickson and Daniel Kahneman's 'peak-end effect.' This research showed that endings matter as we filter our memories according to a 'peak' memory (something exceptionally good – or exceptionally bad) and, crucially, by what we remember of and how we feel about the *ending*.[100]
    - Aristotle's view was that the ending must recapitulate the main points, ignite the audience's emotions and leave a favourable impression of the speaker (their *ethos*). Cicero's recommendations were similar, and he emphasized the importance of the speaker evoking sympathy for their arguments in the conclusion.[101]

Goal: To find the best way to arrange your material.

Guiding question: What order should I use to make my point most effectively?

Action: Arrange ideas in a logical and organized manner that is true to the Golden Thread.

ELOCUTIO (STYLE)

This allows me to raise again one of what I call my 'overarching communications sentiments': that in the communications world – and here I include everything from company, brand and public sector output to speeches, PowerPoints, legal arguments and documents – we devote too much time and intellectual energy to content and not enough to form.

Elocutio deals explicitly with the importance of form, or style. Again, understanding your audience is key, but this is where you can deploy the full panoply of rhetorical devices: from the basics (metaphors, similes and analogies) to alliteration, anaphora (repeating the same word or expression at the beginning of sequences), litotes (using a double negative to emphasize positive meaning, such as "not inconsiderable amount of money") or onomatopoeia (where the sound of the word conjures up meaning).

But it goes without saying that whichever you use, do not drown in them or sacrifice clarity for gratuitous stylization either.

Goal: To find the best way to make your material memorably emotive.

Guiding question: What stylistic devices can I use to make the form more effective?

Action: Work on your content and let the material guide which rhetorical tricks seem most effective, remembering not to let style overwhelm content.

MEMORIA/MEMORY

In ancient times, many of the great orators took the canon of memory literally by actually memorizing their speeches. Although these days we do not need to memorize our works of rhetoric (especially in written form), there are several other ways to incorporate memory when crafting a speech, presentation or essay.

There are several mnemonic exercises that can be usefully deployed. Here is one I use myself and recommend.

It's another use of the magic number three, the favoured cardinal number among communicators of all hues. This simple trick doesn't allow you to memorize something in its entirety, but it can be of great help, both as a mnemonic and as a precaution in case of technological breakdown (the screen fails, doesn't talk to your laptop, etc.).

So, when you are about to give a speech or presentation, make sure beforehand that you:

- Divide your speech or presentation into three parts.

- Give each of the three parts a label to remember it by: a word (or two, but no more than three), an image or a metaphor.

- If you remember those three summary words or images (perhaps employing another rhetorical technique, such as alliteration or forming an acronym), it may be essential in case of that tech crash. But it can also give you confidence and fluency when presenting.

You can find more on this topic by hunting down the idea of the memory palace, a system for remembering catalogues of information that goes back to ancient times but is still used by stage magicians and psychological illusionists.[102]

The concept of the memory palace (also known as the method of loci) allows people to memorize enormous amounts of information by placing images that represent the data into mental locations. It goes all the way back to the 6th- and 5th-century BCE Greek poet Simonides of Ceos, who is said to have first developed the idea of using spatial imagination to retain information.

Cicero and Quintilian each tell their own version of this story, but the gist is that Simonides had just left a dinner party in a stately home when the roof collapsed, crushing all the remaining guests beyond recognition. Because he could recall where each person was sitting when he left, Simonides was able to identify all of their corpses, and in that he recognized the mnemonic power to be found in conjuring mental images of space.

Goal: To use the power of memory to your best advantage.

Guiding question: How can I memorize my Golden Thread to aid fluency and confidence?

Action: Deploy the 'magic number three' and any other rhetorical tricks that work for you.

PRONUNTIATIO (DELIVERY)

More commonly defined as 'presentation skills,' *pronuntiatio* involves careful consideration of when to make eye contact, when to use hand gestures, when to smile, how to 'work the room' and even what to wear.

Emphasis, tone of voice, change of pace, pauses, volume, gesticulation, body language, positioning and props are all tools that can help you effectively deliver your arguments.

Goal: To use the softer skills to make your content even more memorable

Guiding question: Which skills can I deploy – to what effect, and when

Action: Try out and play with the array of skills to take your natural character and personality and bring it more to life.

FUN WITH CICERO

Let's end this section on Cicero with a couple of digressions.

Firstly, one for the grammar geeks – an imagined conversation between Cicero, as prosecutor, and Catiline, a man accused of plotting to overthrow the Roman Republic (we have Cicero's four speeches from 63 BCE):

Cicero: You need to abandon Rome, immediately.
Catiline: Can we please change the subject?
Cicero: Rome needs to be immediately abandoned by you.

Secondly, the legacy of Cicero lives on in strange ways.

One example is that the University of Florida student ambassadors are known as Cicerones, as this is the current Italian word for 'guide.' (The origin of the name seems to be linked to chickpeas.)[103]

THE GREEK ARTS OF PERSUASION AND LOVE

One of the more obscure and elusive of the Greek mythological characters is the goddess Peitho, patron of the arts of persuasion (in Greek, *peitho* means 'persuasion'). This makes her one of the more abstract allegorical figures alongside Tyche (Chance) and Ate (Discord).

As the personified spirit (*daemon*) of persuasion, seduction and charming speech, Peitho was a handmaiden and herald of the goddess Aphrodite.

She is barely cited in any of the standard legends or tales, and remains a mysterious background figure. However, like her Roman counterpart, Suada, she is associated with deception, desire and seduction. She appears in several friezes and on vases, one of which shows her tantalizingly overseeing one of the great seduction scenes in history, between Helen (formerly of Sparta) and Paris, Prince of Troy.

As ever with myth, we can find deep human truths buried not too deeply beneath. The Greeks knew well the power of persuasion and its seductive power. From the story (or myth) of the Trojan War to the advertising titans of Madison Avenue and beyond, the psychological and rhetorical truth is there to behold: persuasion is seduction, sex sells, desire drives demand. Again, the Greeks saw no contradiction between facts and rationality on the one hand, and the raw force of emotion on the other.

The Athenian comic poet Aristophanes often linked politics and love (Eros). A contemporary comic, Eupolis, said that "Peitho sat upon the lips of Pericles," the great leader and communicator of Athens at its glorious heights in the 5th century BCE (in whose mouth the Athenian historian of the Peloponnesian War, Thucydides, puts some of the greatest speeches ever created).

The Greeks held that persuasion wasn't a sin, or to be demeaned, but actually part of each person's civic duty (etymologically, *peitho* is linked to the Latin *fides*, meaning 'faith').

Before we leave Helen of Troy (the face that launched a thousand ships, in Christopher Marlowe's memorable expression from *Doctor Faustus*), we can look to another Greek rhetorician (and philosopher).

Gorgias of Leontini, who we heard about above, wrote an *Encomium of Helen*. It was his showpiece (these days a Hollywood calling card) and in it he explored the function of language in oratory by examining Helen's role in the Trojan myth and finally exculpating her. Gorgias explores four ways in which she might have been persuaded to abandon Sparta and her husband, King Menelaus, and come to Troy: by the gods, by brute force, by love or by speech (*logos*).

Gorgias concludes that she was most likely "struck out of her wits" by Paris's eloquence and thus should be judged blameless:

> Speech is a powerful master, which by means of the finest and most invisible body (sound) has effects that are almost divine.[104]

Recognized by the likes of Aristotle as a coiner of many metaphors, Gorgias goes on to compare the effect of speech on the mind as comparable to the power of drugs on the nature of the body, as though bewitching us with a kind of evil persuasion (he uses the word *peitho* again).

Logos (speech, words, rhetoric, language, reason) for Gorgias is irresistible, and in this he is squarely in the Greek tradition, which saw the likes of Homer revered for his oral gifts. Speech was not only inspiring but also divinely inspired (our word 'enthuse' has *theos*, 'inspired by a god,' at its heart, noted in *Part One*).

> **Stories set out not to persuade, but beguile.**

Philip Pullman

Are the classics still relevant and, if so, how?

PERORATIO

STEALING A MOMENT

Dramatic endings, remember?

So, I'd like to start with a news story about a burglar in Rome from August 2024.[105]

The burglar in question broke into an apartment in Rome and was arrested after pausing in the middle of the robbery to read a book about Greek mythology.

The 38-year-old Italian man had gained access to the building in the Prati district from the balcony, but apparently became so distracted after seeing a book on a bedside table that he sat down to read. The owner of the property woke up and confronted him as the burglar was sitting on a bed fully immersed in the book.

In case you were wondering, the (Italian) book was an analysis of *The Iliad* from the point of view of the gods themselves, called *The Gods at Six o'Clock:* The Iliad *at Cocktail Time* by Italian poet and writer Giovanni Nucci. (There may be a linguistic nuance gone AWOL in the translation.)[106]

While I would never endorse any form of illegal behaviour, I do hope the defence used the burglar's passion for Greek mythology to mitigate his sentence.

LOCUS CLASSICUS

As I said at the start (*exordium*), in my 'oeuvre', I am constantly striving to introduce new impetus and ideas into the world of marketing and communications to shake it out of its comfortable assumptions. Examples include storytelling, to remind us not to bombard people with dry, cold, passionless facts; behavioural economics, to ensure that our brand and content are led by emotion and appreciate the power of System 1 thinking; and pursuit of the holy grail of insight, to help us recognize the power of creative serendipity and of forging unconscious connections into new combinations.

So here, I have explored how using the enormous body of ideas handed down to us in the form of 'the classics' can help us generate new ideas, approaches and ways of thinking to accomplish those goals. Because if that enormous body of literature, philosophy, history and science (some estimates reckon we only have 1% of what was produced in antiquity) can't teach us something new, well, we are missing something.

In the words of Rafał Toczko, assistant professor in the Department of Classics at Nicolaus Copernicus University in Toruń, Poland, on the classics website Antigone (which numbers Stephen Fry among its contributors):

> The achievements of the Greeks and Romans in the field of literature, art and ideas were, and still are, a principal source of our intellectual, aesthetic and spiritual energy.[107]

I am not advocating for a return to the past where classics was on every public school curriculum, embedded as it often was in a set of outdated patrician values that were at the heart (in the UK, at least) of the British Empire and the system that sustained it. But, if classics are divorced from that context, surely we can still see the value of exploring this enormous wealth of material?

Toczko again:

> In former ages, the Classical tradition (in a narrower sense) influenced almost every new literary or political work in the Western world: there would be no modern state if Voltaire, Benjamin Franklin or John Adams had not known and value[d] the works of Cicero; there would be no Leonardo da Vinci or Copernicus without Hellenistic science; there would be no national epics without Virgil; there would be no Racine without Euripides and Seneca, no Shakespeare without Ovid or Plutarch. ... The reflections of Marcus Aurelius can help us no less than the works of popular 'life coaches,' and ancient comedies turn out to be no less funny than many modern movies or plays, so long as we read them attentively, and stage them with skill.

IN FINE

So, what can we take, learn and deploy from the classics in our day-to-day marketing and comms world?

BE MORE FOX?

There is a plethora* of occasions when we can avail ourselves of Archilochus' 'hedgehog and fox' metaphor.

At the 'meta' level, it invites us to question whether we wish to subscribe to one grand theory of everything (as physicists seek) or are happy to eclectically use a number of theories and approaches. For all my advancement of storytelling and evangelizing of behavioural economics, I am still happy to advocate for a variety of methodologies rather than putting all of my ideological eggs in the same basket.

At the least, it's a great metaphor or story for use in presentations, speeches, or any form of debate and discussion: who are you and what would you rather be – a hedgehog (one big idea) or a fox (who knows many things)? It can be a way of contrasting different approaches to business, to management or even to HR (recruitment: is the best team a mixture of hedgehogs and foxes?!).

It can also be deployed when talking about your brand and its UX (user experience), or your comms or media strategy (one big idea or many smaller ideas).

At the brand positioning level, it can be a useful frame of reference for discussing your overall brand platform among your colleagues and agencies. Specifically, should your brand have a hedgehog comms idea (one grand overarching vision or idea, or what was once called a BHAG – big hairy audacious goal)? Or is it better to invest your time and budget in smaller, more fox-like benefits, messages and small-scale human communications? (Behavioural economics suggests that sometimes these small, personal, human details can be more enduring and meaningful.)

In the world of presentations, as a confirmed storyteller, I would suggest that a good deck or speech should aim for the hedgehog approach – having a central Golden Thread, which the brain can latch onto and retain, rather than setting loose a skulk (yes, I know: me neither) of foxes to cause havoc with the synapses of your audience.

And in any event, it is a simple, elegant, universal visual metaphor that can be adapted to so many occasions and channels

(*Plethora, from the Greek meaning 'fullness.' Linked to 'complete,' 'replete,' 'deplete' and all the 'plus' words – e.g. surplus, nonplus and words beginning with 'poly.')

TIMELESS MYTHS

As we saw earlier myths and stories are as Sallustius described them: they may never have happened in the specific, but they are eternal in their capacity to teach and instruct us with moral clarity.

THE MYTH	THE THREAD OF TRUTH	THE MORAL
1. PHAETHON, PROMETHEUS, ICARUS	HUBRIS: ARROGANCE, AMBITION AND LOSS OF CONTROL	• DON'T ASSUME CONTROL AND MASTERY • TAKE ADVICE FROM ELDERS • AVOID RASHNESS
2. SISYPHUS	RELENTLESSNESS	• HOWEVER APPARENTLY FUTILE, WE KEEP ON PUSHING THAT BOULDER • THE POWER OF RESILIENCE
3. DIONYSUS VS APOLLO	EMOTIONS BALANCE RATIONALITY	• RATIONALITY MUST NOT STRANGLE EMOTION, CREATIVITY OR FREEDOM • BE MORE DIONYSUS (AND LESS PENTHEUS)
4. ACHILLES	NOBILITY AND VIRTUE (OCCASIONALLY VEERING INTO STUBBORNNESS)	• BE STEADFAST, LOYAL AND VIRTUOUS (EVEN IF THOSE AROUND YOU AREN'T)
5. ODYSSEUS	CUNNING AND DEVIOUSNESS	• LIFE IS A JOURNEY – YOU NEED TO BE ARTFUL AND COMPLICATED
6. PROTEUS	WE ARE ALL A COLLECTION OF 'MANY MES'	• NEVER UNDERESTIMATE HUMAN COMPLEXITY
7. HERACLITUS	EVERYTHING CHANGES	• PEOPLE CHANGE

There are many ways in which an appreciation of these myths can help us in our general business, marketing and communications. So, consider how you can deploy the myths we explored there.

THE APPLICATION(S)	POSITIVES/NEGATIVES
• INTRODUCING NEW IDEAS TO THE C-SUITE • INTRODUCING NEW PRODUCTS INTO THE MARKET WITHOUT TESTING • SPEAKING TO YOUR COLLEAGUES ABOUT COLLABORATION • TECH AND AI (THESE ARE ESPECIALLY RELEVANT)	+ ALL BREAKTHROUGHS NEED SOME HUBRIS + MAVERICKS NEED TO GO WITH THEIR GUT, NOT RELY ON ASKING CONSUMERS WHAT THEY WANT - RISK OF DEVOLVING INTO CHAOS
• RALLYING THE TEAM BEFORE OR AFTER A CORPORATE RESTRUCTURE • GENERAL TEAM- BUILDING EVENTS	+ NOTHING IS GAINED WITHOUT PAIN: BUILD RESILIENCE - SOMETIMES, THE ROCK WILL JUST KEEP COMING DOWN - HAVE YOU GOT THE EFFORT AND PATIENCE?
• ENSURING YOUR BRAND, COMMS, UX OR TEAM DO NOT UNDERESTIMATE EMOTION • HUNDREDS OF OTHER APPLICATIONS	+ BEHAVIOURAL ECONOMICS REMINDS US TO ALWAYS ADDRESS EMOTIONS AND SYSTEM 1 - IGNORE EMOTIONS AT YOUR PERIL
• ENSURING YOUR COMPANY AND COMMUNICATIONS ARE PRINCIPLED • BEING HONEST, TRANSPARENT AND AUTHENTIC	+ BELIEF AND PRINCIPLES MATTER - ... AS LONG AS THEY DON'T TEND TOWARD PIG-HEADEDNESS - DON'T COMPROMISE THE TEAM
• PREPARING FOR THE UNEXPECTED - THERE MAY BE SIRENS OR A CYCLOPS AROUND THE CORNER ...	+ EVERY JOURNEY CAN BE UNPREDICTABLE: PLAN FOR IT AS MUCH AS YOU CAN - DON'T TRY TO BE TOO DEVIOUS
• DON'T ASSUME YOUR STAKEHOLDERS OR CONSUMERS ARE ALL MONOLITHICALLY SIMPLE AND PREDICTABLE	+ VERSATILITY IS KEY - AVOID PEOPLE WHO ARE SLIPPERY AND EVASIVE
• BEWARE OSSIFIED SEGMENTATIONS • REMEMBER THAT AS COMPANIES CHANGE, PEOPLE AND CULTURE ALSO CHANGE	+ CHANGE IS THE ONLY CONSTANT ... - ... BUT CHANGE IS STRANGE: EXPECT BUMPS

FIGURE 2

Here are a few options:

- Consider using a myth as a story thread or metaphor that can hold your argument, speech or presentation together. For example, if you are talking tech, any of the stories mentioned in *Part One* and illustrated in *Figure 2* can be a memorable way of summarizing and expressing the core idea of your argument (whichever end of the hedgehog–fox spectrum you prefer: unbridled genius or uncontrolled chaos).

- If you are giving a talk to the troops in the office, why not dispense with the PowerPoint full of solutionizing, synergizing and reaching out – and tell a story using a myth or fable?

- If you want to test your oratorical skills, consider finding a myth or character and using that as the basis for your talk. For example, how might you learn from the brand mythologies found in *Part One*, for Virgin, Nike, Sennheiser, Duravit and the Royal Albert Hall?

As a first step, examine *Figure 2*: a selection of the myths, what they mean and some ways in which you can use them.

TEACH RHETORIC

After watching the Obamas perform (and it was quite the performance) at the Democratic National Convention in Chicago in August 2024, it would have been hard for anyone to deny the power of rhetoric and its role at the centre of public life. The ability to captivate a crowd, to seamlessly blend anecdote, joke, story and light roasting of your opponent tempered with just enough political nous and substance – this is a rare feat, especially for a couple.

Rhetoric has often been (perhaps can even be defined as) a public act of effectiveness. So, whether it is a matter of a conference speech, a talk to your team, a document, a pitch or a quarterly update via PowerPoint, one of your central aims has to be to persuade a public, an audience.

Rhetoric, in the words of the classicist and teacher of rhetoric George A. Kennedy, is "the energy inherent in emotion and thought."[108]

For Tania Smith, professor of rhetorical theory, criticism and history at the University of Calgary, "rhetoric is the study and practice of communication that persuades, informs, inspires, or entertains target audiences in order to change or reinforce beliefs, values, habits or actions."[109]

THE MODERN TRIVIUM

Just as I ended *The Consumer Behaviour Book* with a plea to teach behaviour change thinking to pupils and students, so that we can all be aware of the tools that governments, political parties and big companies use to persuade and influence us, I would like to canvas for the teaching of rhetoric for much the same reasons.

Perhaps education systems around the world could introduce a new trivium (shorn of some of its more arcane trappings: reframing it by not calling it a trivium would probably help to popularize it).

Rather than grammar, rhetoric and logic, may I suggest schools offer something along the lines of the Art and Science of Influence (ASI, if it needs a justificatory acronym). *Figure 3* shows the three areas ASI could contain.

THE ART AND SCIENCE OF INFLUENCE

BEHAVIOURAL ECONOMICS
EVOLUTIONARY PSYCHOLOGY
NEUROSCIENCE
COMPLEXITY THEORY

CLASSICAL RHETORIC
PUBLIC SPEAKING
STORYTELLING

ADVERTISING THEORY
POLITICAL COMMUNICATION
ETHICS

FIGURE 3

Firstly, it would involve an appreciation of behavioural economics, neuroscience and evolutionary psychology (the science), but also the power of rhetoric as discussed here (more of the art).

Storytelling would be the second element. As I hope to have demonstrated in my other books, storytelling remains our universal operating system (apologies for the computer metaphor) as it is both natural and universal to our species and still (at the time of writing) something that AI has not caught up with (at least not yet at the time of writing).

But a full appreciation of the way the forces of rhetoric and influence are brought to bear on us as citizens (not just as consumers) must also explore the ways that experts in the field of communication use their knowledge.

This would include an in-depth analysis of how advertising works, looking at some of the great creative geniuses from Bernbach and Ogilvy, and those from the ad sector and beyond who have tried to analyse, codify or understand theories of persuasion. This would be appealingly effortless for younger members of society, who are so acclimatized to advertising and communications that they have strong opinions on 'what I like' (maybe even 'what works'). But it would also give them a grounding on why those ads look the way they do, what they are trying to accomplish (the comms 101 of who they are trying to appeal to and how: targeting and strategy). My lecturing at various universities confirms that students lap this up.

One area that would be given special attention is that of political communication. Here, ASI would delve into the ways that governments, political parties, and other special interest groups and activists use the techniques of persuasion to gain our attention and attempt to sway us in their direction. Every ASI student would be given a copy of Drew Westen's insightful book *The Political Brain* (its subtitle – *The Role of Emotion in Deciding the Fate of the Nation* – gives the merest hint of the political analysis within).[110]

And finally, there would have to be a module on ethics – again based on an understanding of behavioural economics (informed by the works of people like Jonathan Haidt) and digging both into the areas where ethical dilemmas may be confronted head on and those where ethics is a secondary or irrelevant matter.

ENDNOTES

1. See Howard Wainer and Shaun Lysen, "That's Funny..." *American Scientist* 97 (4) (2009), https://www.americanscientist.org/article/thats-funny.

2. A. K. Blakemore, "Glorious Exploits by Ferdia Lennon Review - Classical Tragedy as a Celtic Caper," (The Guardian), last modified 6 January 2024, https://www.theguardian.com/books/2024/jan/06/glorious-exploits-by-ferdia-lennon-review-classical-tragedy-as-a-celtic-caper.

3. The Associated Press, "That's No Pizza: A Wall Painting Found in Pompeii Doesn't Depict Italy's Iconic Dish," (*NPR*), last modified 28 June 2023, https://www.npr.org/2023/06/28/1184724633/pizza-a-wall-painting-pompeii; Rachel Roddy, "'It Smelled Like Toffee Apples': How I Recreated the 2,000-Year-Old Pompeii Pizza," (*The Guardian*), last modified 1 July 2023, https://www.theguardian.com/food/2023/jul/01/how-i-recreated-the-pompeii-pizza-smelled-like-toffee-apples.

4. As shared by Mary Beard on X, 2 July 2024: https://twitter.com/wmarybeard/status/1808034339193524542.

5. Evan Osnos, "Can Mark Zuckerberg Fix Facebook Before It Breaks Democracy?" (*The New Yorker*), last modified 10 September 2018, https://www.newyorker.com/magazine/2018/09/17/can-mark-zuckerberg-fix-facebook-before-it-breaks-democracy.

6. https://www.theverge.com/2024/9/25/24254262/zuck-or-nothing.

7. Kieran Corcoran, "Zuck's Birthday T-Shirt Is a Tribute to ANCIENT ROME, Facebook's History, and Going Hard," (*Business Insider*), last modified 15 May 2024, https://www.businessinsider.com/mark-zuckerberg-carthago-delenda-est-latin-t-shirt-explained-2024-5.

8. "The Economist's Word of the Year for 2024," (*The Economist*), last modified 29 November 2024, https://www.economist.com/culture/2024/11/29/the-economists-word-of-the-year-for-2024; Matthew Cantor, "'Government by the Worst': Why People Are Calling Trump's New Sidekicks a 'Kakistocracy,'" (*The Guardian*), last modified 21 November 2024, https://www.theguardian.com/us-news/2024/nov/21/trump-administration-kakistocracy; Beppe Severgnini, "American Kakistocracy," (*The Atlantic*), last modified 16 November, 2024, https://www.theatlantic.com/politics/archive/2024/11/american-kakistocracy-donald-trump-berlusconi/680675; "Kakistocracy," Google Trends data October 2024 to March 2025, accessed 30 March 2025, https://trends.google.com/trends/explore?date=2024-10-01%202025-03-30&geo=US&q=%2Fg%2F121sx80g&hl=en-GB. In other words, as Nancy Friedman wrote at her language blog *Fritinancy* on 5 December 2016, "you could say that *kakistocracy* is 'government by the shitty,'" https://nancyfriedman.typepad.com/away_with_words/2016/12/word-of-the-week-kakistocracy.html.

9. Isaiah Berlin, *The Hedgehog and The Fox* (London: Weidenfeld & Nicolson, 1953). See also Philip E. Tetlock, *Expert Political Judgement* (Princeton: Princeton University Press, 2005) and John Kay, *Obliquity: Why Our Goals Are Best Achieved Indirectly* (London: Profile Books, 2010).

10. Daniel Kahneman, *Thinking, Fast and Slow* (New York: Farrar, Straus and Giroux, 2011).

11. See Louis Menand, "Everybody's an Expert," (*The New Yorker*), last modified 27 November 2005, https://www.newyorker.com/magazine/2005/12/05/everybodys-an-expert.

12. Nate Silver, *The Signal and The Noise* (New York: Penguin, 2012).

13. John Kay and Mervyn King, *Radical Uncertainty: Decision-making for an Unknowable Future* (London: Bridge Street Press, 2020); Edward Chancellor, "Breakingviews – Chancellor: A Catastrophic Failure of Risk Control," (Reuters), last modified 5 June 2020, https://www.reuters.com/article/breakingviews/breakingviews-chancellor-a-catastrophic-failure-of-risk-control-idUSKBN23C0XK.

14. Carol S. Dweck, *Mindset: The New Psychology of Success* (New York: Random House, 2006).

15. Lord Saatchi, *Brutal Simplicity of Thought* (London: Ebury Press, 2011).

16. Tristan S. Taylor, "Caesar's Gallic Genocide," in *The Cambridge World History of Genocide*, vol. 1, eds. Ben Kiernan, T. M. Lemos and Tristan S. Taylor (Cambridge: Cambridge University Press, 2023).

17. Vanessa Barford, "Why Do Some People Refer to Themselves in the Third Person?" (*BBC News*), last modified 28 August 2015, https://www.bbc.co.uk/news/magazine-33943762.

18. Ben Okri, *A Way of Being Free* (London: Head of Zeus, 2015).

19. Adam Nicolson, *The Mighty Dead: Why Homer Matters* (London: William Collins, 2014).

20. Luc Ferry, *The Wisdom of the Myths: How Greek Mythology Can Change Your Life* (New York: Harper Perennial, 2014).

21. For more on Sallustius, see my book *InCitations: Discovering a World of Inspiration through Quotes, Words and Expressions* (London: LID Publishing, 2020).

22. Oren Harman, *Evolutions: Fifteen Myths that Explain Our World* (London: Apollo, 2018).

23. Harman, *Evolutions*.

24. Matthew Stewart, *The Management Myth: Why the Experts Keep Getting It Wrong* (London: W. W. Norton, 2009).

25. "The Education Hub: Myth Busting," (*Gov.uk*), last modified 19 August 2022, https://educationhub.blog.gov.uk/category/myth-busting; "Coronavirus Disease (COVID-19) Advice for the Public: Mythbusters," (*World Health Organization*), last modified 19 January 2022, https://www.who.int/emergencies/diseases/novel-coronavirus-2019/advice-for-public/myth-busters.

26. Bill Bryson, *Made in America* (New York: Secker & Warburg, 1994).

27. Douglas Adams, *The Hitchhiker's Guide to the Galaxy* (London: Pan, 1979).

28. "How Richard Branson Started His First Business Out of a Phone Booth," (*Inc.*), last modified 28 June 2016, https://www.inc.com/richard-branson/how-he-started-his-first-business-out-of-a-phone-booth.html;

Rachel Gregg, "Sir Richard Branson on Becoming an Entrepreneur (by Accident)," (*Creative Live*), last modified 6 December 2017, https://www.creativelive.com/blog/chase-jarvis-interviews-sir-richard-branson.

29. Rachel Gregg, "Sir Richard Branson on Becoming an Entrepreneur (by Accident)," (*Creative Live*), last modified 6 December 2017, https://www.creativelive.com/blog/chase-jarvis-interviews-sir-richard-branson.

30. Hayley Peterson, "The Bizarre Inspiration Behind Nike's First Pair of Running Shoes," (*Business Insider*), last modified 6 July 2015, https://www.businessinsider.com/nikes-first-running-shoes-were-made-in-a-waffle-iron-2015-7; "Never Done Breaking the Mould," (*Nike*), last modified 17 May 2022, https://www.nike.com/gb/a/never-done-breaking-the-mold-the-waffle-mindset.

31. Hayley Peterson, "The Bizarre Inspiration Behind Nike's First Pair of Running Shoes," (*Business Insider*), last modified 6 July 2015, www.businessinsider.com/nikes-first-running-shoes-were-made-in-a-waffle-iron-2015-7.

32. See https://www.duravit.co.uk.

33. Kate Fox, *Watching the English: The Hidden Rules of English Behaviour* (London: Hodder & Stoughton, 2005).

34. Daniel Kahneman, *Thinking, Fast and Slow* (New York: Farrar, Straus and Giroux, 2011).

35. Charles Handy, *Gods of Management* (London: Pan, 1985); "A Selection from among the Names and Epithets of Dionysos," (*Hermetic Fellowship*), accessed 30 March 2025, http://www.hermeticfellowship.org/Dionysion/Godnames.html; "Dionysos Titles," (*Theoi*), accessed 30 March 2025, http://www.theoi.com/Cult/DionysosTitles.html.

36. James George Frazer, *The Golden Bough* (London: Macmillan, 1890).

37. Emily Wilson (trans. and ed.), *The Odyssey* (New York: W. W. Norton, 2017).

38. Marcel Proust, *A la Recherche du Temps Perdu*, vol. 2 (), 299.

39. Daniel C. Dennett, *Consciousness Explained* (New York: Little, Brown, 1991).

40. Julian Baggini, *The Ego Trick* (London: Granta, 2011).

41. Woody Allen, "The Kugelmass Episode," in *Side Effects* (New York: Random House, 1980), first published in *The New Yorker* in 1977.

42. Virginia Valentine and Wendy Gordon, "The 21st Century Consumer: A New Model of Thinking," *International Journal of Market Research*, 42 (2) (2000): 1–16.

43. Yuval Noah Harari, *Nexus: A Brief History of Information Networks from the Stone Age to AI* (London: Fern Press, 2024); Yuval Noah Harari, "'Never Summon a Power You Can't Control': Yuval Noah Harari on How AI Could Threaten Democracy and Divide the World," (*The Guardian*), last modified 24 August 2024, https://www.theguardian.com/technology/article/2024/aug/24/yuval-noah-harari-ai-book-extract-nexus.

44. "The Fate of Phaeton," (*History Today*), last modified September 2018, https://www.historytoday.com/archive/foundations/fate-phaeton.

45. Adrienne Mayor, "Prometheus' Toolbox: Human Life as Technology from Greek Mythology to Mary Shelley's *Frankenstein*," (*Lapham's Quarterly*), accessed 30 March 2025, https://www.laphamsquarterly.org/technology/prometheus-toolbox; see also "Prometheus: Stealing Fire from the Gods," (*National Museums Liverpool*), accessed 30 March 2025, https://www.liverpoolmuseums.org.uk/world-museum/greek-myths-and-legends/prometheus-stealing-fire-gods.

46. John Baker, "Prime Minister Boris Johnson Played Prometheus During Recovery from Covid Virus," (*Wiltshire Times*), last modified 29 October 2021, https://www.wiltshiretimes.co.uk/news/19680837.prime-minister-boris-johnson-played-prometheus-recovery-covid-virus.

47. See https://github.com/codeincrypt/prometheus-grafana.

48. Philip McCouat, "Bruegel's *Icarus* and the Perils of Flight," (*Journal of Art in Society*), last modified 2019, https://www.artinsociety.com/perception-and-blindness-in-the-16th-century-667243.html.

49. "The Surprising Origin of the 'Genie Is Out of the Bottle' Saying," (*Origin of Genies*), accessed 30 March 2025, https://originofgenies.wordpress.com/2023/01/16/the-surprising-origin-of-the-genie-is-out-of-the-bottle-saying.

50. First published in English by Hamish Hamilton in 1955.

51. Mark Brown, "Jackie Weaver Had 'No Authority' After All, Investigation Finds," (*The Guardian*), last modified 29 March 2022, https://www.theguardian.com/society/2022/mar/29/jackie-weaver-had-no-authority-after-all-investigation-finds; Lauren Hirst, "Jackie Weaver: Viral Star Enjoying Her Celebrity 'Adventure,'" (*BBC News*), last modified 25 December 2021, https://www.bbc.co.uk/news/uk-england-manchester-59745618.

52. See "Stephen King 1971: What Is a Brand?" (*Campaign*), last modified 5 October 2007, https://www.campaignlive.co.uk/article/stephen-king-1971-brand/743160.

53. "Metaphysics" (*Merriam-Webster*), accessed 30 March 2025, https://www.merriam-webster.com/dictionary/metaphysics.

54. Bethany Williams, "The Ship of Theseus Thought Experiment: An Ancient Paradox," (*The Collector*), last modified 8 July 2021, https://www.thecollector.com/the-ship-of-theseus; S. Marc Cohen, "Identity, Persistence, and the Ship of Theseus," (*Philosophy 320: History of Ancient Philosophy, University of Washington*), last modified 6 October 2004, https://faculty.washington.edu/smcohen/320/theseus.html.

55. Tor Nørretranders, *The User Illusion*, trans. Jonathan Sydenham (London: Allen Lane, 1998); "Exformation," (*World Wide Words*), last modified 26 October 1998, https://www.worldwidewords.org/tp-exf1.html.

56. William Calvin, *The Cerebral Code: Thinking a Thought in the Mosaics of the Mind* (Cambridge, MA: MIT Press, 1998); William Calvin and Derek Bickerton, *Lingua ex Machina: Reconciling Darwin and Chomsky with the Human Brain* (Cambridge, MA: MIT Press, 2001).

57. Richard Dawkins, *Unweaving the Rainbow: Science, Delusion and the Appetite for Wonder* (London: Penguin, 1998).

58. Andrew Ehrenberg, Neil Barnard and John Scriven, "Differentiation or Salience," *Journal of Advertising Research*, last modified November/December 1997, https://www.warc.com/fulltext/JAR/9076.htm.

59. Niles Eldredge and S. J. Gould, "Punctuated Equilibria: An Alternative to Phyletic Gradualism," in *Models in Paleobiology*, ed. T. J. M. Schopf (San Francisco: Freeman Cooper, 1972).

60. E. O. Wilson, *Consilience: The Unity of Knowledge* (London: Little, Brown, 1998).

61. "Resilience," (*Etymonline*), accessed 30 March 2025, https://www.etymonline.com/word/resilience.

62. "Resilience," Google Ngram data 1800 to 2022, accessed 30 March 2025, https://books.google.com/ngrams/graph?content=resilience&year_start=1800&year_end=2022&corpus=en&smoothing=3.

63. "Decimate" (Etymonline), accessed 30 March 2025, https://www.etymonline.com/search?q=decimate.

64. Christine Spier, "Thumbs Up or Thumbs Down? Looking at Gérôme's 'Pollice Verso,'" (*Getty*), last modified 6 August 2010, https://blogs.getty.edu/iris/thumbs-up-or-thumbs-down-looking-at-geromes-pollice-verso; Merrill Fabry, "Where Does the 'Thumbs-Up' Gesture Really Come From?" (*Time*), last modified 25 October 2017, https://time.com/4984728/thumbs-up-thumbs-down-history.

65. Anthony Corbeill, *Nature Embodied: Gesture in Ancient Rome* (Princeton: Princeton University Press, 2003).

66. "Cosmetic," (*Etymonline*), accessed 30 March 2025, https://www.etymonline.com/word/cosmetic.

67. "Notions of Leisure: From Otium to Wellness," (*Guggenheim*), accessed 30 March 2025, https://www.guggenheim.org/teaching-materials/countryside-the-future/notions-of-leisure-from-otium-to-wellness; Gaia Paradiso, "The Importance of Otium and Thermae, Cultural (S) places for Socialization and Body Caring," (*Huffpost*), last modified 30 December 2017, https://www.huffpost.com/entry/the-importance-of-otium-thermae-cultural-splaces_b_5a478d1de4b0d86c803c76f0.

68. Horace, *Odes*, II, 16.

69. "Jan 10, 49 BC: Caesar Crosses the Rubicon," (*National Geographic*), accessed 30 March 2025, https://education.nationalgeographic.org/resource/caesar-crosses-rubicon; N. S. Gill, "Meaning Behind the Phrase to Cross the Rubicon," (*Thought Co.*), last modified 15 July 2019, https://www.thoughtco.com/meaning-cross-the-rubicon-117548;

Alan Newman, "Crossing the Rubicon," (*Atlas Obscura*), accessed 30 March 2025, https://www.atlasobscura.com/places/crossing-the-rubicon; Alyssa Kotva, "Julius Caesar Crosses the Rubicon," (*Origins*), last modified January 2024, https://origins.osu.edu/read/julius-caesar-crosses-rubicon.

70. Martin Gayford, "Gerhard Richter: Behind the Pictures," (*The Telegraph*), last modified 20 September 2008, https://www.telegraph.co.uk/culture/art/3561020/Gerhard-Richter-behind-the-pictures.html.

71. Steve Rosenberg, "Russia's Targeting of 'Enemies Within' Evokes Ghosts of the Soviet Past," (*BBC News*), last modified 13 September 2024, https://www.bbc.co.uk/news/articles/c3ejk4p3jxjo.

72. Jacquelyn Cafasso, "Hemopneumothorax," (*Healthline*), last modified 18 September 2018, https://www.healthline.com/health/hemopneumothorax.

73. "Bossi: 'Sono Porci Questi Romani,'" (*La Repubblica*), last modified 27 September 2010, https://www.repubblica.it/politica/2010/09/27/video/bossi_sono_porci_questi_romani-422679971.

74. Philip Collins, *When They Go Low, We Go High* (London: 4th Estate, 2017).

75. See also Bryant Girouard, "Gorgias," in *Open Rhetoric: A Collaborative History of Rhetorical Theory and Practice* (PressBooks), accessed 30 March 2025, https://pressbooks.pub/openrhetoric/chapter/gorgias-text.

76. See also Jesús R. Velasco, "Prologue to a Tragedy," (*Iberian Connections*), last modified 2019, https://iberian-connections.yale.edu/articles/aristoteles-latinus-prologue-to-a-tragedy.

77. Aristophanes, "The Clouds," c 423 BCE.

78. Erec Smith, "The Theory and Practice of Rhetoric: An Interview," (*Cato Institute*), last modified 18 May 2023, https://www.cato.org/blog/theory-practice-rhetoric-interview; see also R. C. Jebb, "Rhetoric," (*1902 Encyclopedia*), accessed 30 March 2025, https://www.1902encyclopedia.com/R/RHE/rhetoric.html.

79. "What Is the Trivium and How Does it Apply to Homeschooling?" (*Classical Conversations*), accessed 30 March 2025, https://classicalconversations.com/blog/what-is-the-trivium.

80. Quoted at "Trivium and Quadrivium," (*Liberal Arts*), accessed 30 March 2025, https://liberalarts.online/trivium-and-quadrivium.

81. Sister Miriam Joseph, in *The Trivium: The Liberal Arts of Logic, Grammar, and Rhetoric* (Philadelphia: Paul Dry Books, 2002).

82. From Chapter 3 in "Selections from *An Essay Concerning Human Understanding*, Book 3: By John Locke," ed. Jack Lynch, accessed 30 March 2025, https://jacklynch.net/Texts/locke-language.html.

83. Ezra Pound, "Vorticism," *The Fortnightly Review* n.s. 96 (1 September 1914), https://fortnightlyreview.co.uk/vorticism.

84. Truthiness: Stephen Colbert, *The Colbert Report* (first aired 2005).

85. "Spinning the Tale of 'Spin Doctor,'" (*Merriam-Webster*), accessed 30 March 2025, https://www.merriam-webster.com/wordplay/word-history-spin-doctor; "What's the Meaning of the Phrase 'Spin Doctor'?" (*Phrase Finder*), accessed 30 March 2025, https://www.phrases.org.uk/meanings/spin-doctor.html.

86. Richard H. Thaler and Cass Sunstein, *Nudge: Improving Decisions about Health, Wealth and Happiness* (London: Penguin, 2008).

87. Plato, *Phaedrus*, c 370 BCE.

88. "Sophist," (*Merriam-Webster*), accessed 30 March 2025, https://www.merriam-webster.com/dictionary/sophist; "Sophist," (*Cambridge Dictionary*), accessed 30 March 2025, https://dictionary.cambridge.org/dictionary/english/sophist.

89. "Sophistication," (*Etymonline*), accessed 30 March 2025, https://www.etymonline.com/word/sophistication.

90. Cicero, *De Oratore*, II, 178.

91. Katharina Volk, "Should You Be Upset? Cicero on the Desirability of Emotions," (*Antigone Journal*), accessed 30 March 2025, https://antigonejournal.com/2022/01/cicero-emotion.

92. "Docere debitum est, delectare honorarium, permovere necessarium," *De Optimo Genere Oratorum*, I, 3. Cicero gives the same threefold aims as "ut probet, ut delectet, ut flectet" in *Orator*, 69, and in *De Oratore*, II, 121. See also Donald Lemen Clark, *Rhetoric and Poetry in the*

Renaissance: A Study of Rhetorical Terms in English Renaissance Literary Criticism (New York: Columbia University Press, 1922), n316.

93. "The 5 Canons of Rhetoric," (*Tayla Lawson*), accessed 30 March 2025, https://taylalawson.wordpress.com/about-me; "What Are the Five Canons of Rhetoric?" (*Classical Conversations*), accessed 30 March 2025, https://classicalconversations.com/blog/five-canons-of-rhetoric.

94. Richard Nordquist, "The Parts of a Speech in Classical Rhetoric," (*Thought Co.*), last modified 19 November 2019, https://www.thoughtco.com/parts-of-a-speech-rhetoric-1691589; "A Classical Structure for Composition," (*Learn English or Starve*), last modified 6 March 2015, https://learnenglishorstarve.wordpress.com/2015/03/06/classical-composition-structure.

95. Philip Pullman, "The Path Through the Woods," in *Daemon Voices: On Stories and Storytelling* (Oxford: David Fickling Books, 2017); David Mamet, "Where Do I Point the Camera?" in *On Directing Film* (New York: Penguin, 1991).

96. "Quintilian: *Institutio Oratoria*," (*Penelope, University of Chicago*), last modified 27 October 2017, https://penelope.uchicago.edu/Thayer/E/Roman/Texts/Quintilian/Institutio_Oratoria/home.html.

97. Cicero, *De Oratore*.

98. Cicero, *De Oratore*; Quintilian, *Institutio Oratoria*.

99. Cicero, *De Oratore*.

100. Barbara L. Fredrickson and Daniel Kahneman, "Duration Neglect in Retrospective Evaluations of Affective Episodes," *Journal of Personality and Social Psychology*, 65 (1) (1993): 45–55.

101. Aristotle, *Rhetoric*; Cicero, *De Oratore*.

102. Laura Miller, "Remembering Frances Yates," (*Slate*), last modified 23 November 2015, https://slate.com/culture/2015/11/the-art-of-memory-by-frances-yates-the-historian-who-recovered-the-story-of-simonides-memory-palace.html; "Simonides of Ceos and the Method of Loci," (*Art of Memory*), last modified 4 April 2023, https://artofmemory.com/blog/simonides-of-ceos.

103. "A Brief History," (*Florida Cicerones Alumni Association*), accessed 30 March 2025, https://www.ciceronesalumni.org/history.

104. Gorgias of Leontini, *Encomium of Helen*.

105. Zahra Fatima, "Suspected Burglar Caught after Sitting Down with Book," (*BBC News*), 24 August 2024, https://www.bbc.co.uk/news/articles/cvg4kpv3p4zo.

106. Giovanni Nucci, *Gli dèi alle sei: L'Iliade all'ora dell'aperitivo* (Milan: Bompiani, 2023).

107. Rafał Toczko, "Why Should We Save the Classical Tradition?" (*Antigone*), accessed 30 March 2025, https://antigonejournal.com/2022/02/why-save-classical-tradition.

108. George Kennedy, "A Hoot in the Dark," *Philosophy & Rhetoric*, 25 (1) (1992): 1–21.

109. Tania Smith, "What Is Rhetoric?" (*Edu*Rhetor*), accessed 30 March 2025, https://edurhetor.wordpress.com/about/rhetoric.

110. Drew Westen, *The Political Brain: The Role of Emotion in Deciding the Fate of the Nation* (New York: PublicAffairs, 2007).

ACKNOWLEDGEMENTS

Thanks as ever to Martin for stalwart *dignitas* and *gravitas* over a full decade (yes) and to Nikki and the kids for their thankless patience over the same period.

And to Aiyana for suffering through the edits with her usual *otium*.

Also, to all the classicists who have inspired and continue to inspire me with their *auctoritas*, from Nigel Wilson at Lincoln College, Oxford, to Mary Beard, Bettany Hughes and Natalie Haynes.

ABOUT THE AUTHOR

Anthony "Tas" Tasgal is a man of many lanyards: trainer, author, TEDx speaker, brand/comms strategist and lecturer.

He is a course director for the Chartered Institute of Marketing, the Market Research Society, the Institute of Internal Communication, the Civil Service College and the Chartered Institute of Procurement and Supply.

He is a global speaker, did his first TEDx talk in Newcastle in November 2023 and regularly reviews the papers live on TalkTV.

He specializes in storytelling, behavioural economics and insightment – and, as a lapsed classicist, he also indulges in etymology and Homer (not the yellow one).

He also runs *The Guardian*'s masterclass "Harness the Power of Storytelling to Transform Your Communications" and is a brand ambassador for Home Grown Club in London (https://homegrownclub.co.uk).

He works for clients as varied as the BBC, Nokia, Panasonic, the Royal Albert Hall, EE, Boehringer Ingelheim Animal Health, the Intellectual Property Office (part of the UK government), ReLondon and the NHS.

He is the author of the award-winning *The Storytelling Book*, which has sold nearly 40,000 copies globally (2015), *The Inspiratorium* (2018), *InCitations* (2020), *The Storytelling Workbook* (2022) and *The Insight Book* (2023).

His sixth book, *The Consumer Behaviour Book*, was published in June 2024.

BY THE SAME AUTHOR

ISBN: 978-1-911687-97-9

ISBN: 978-1-911687-38-2

ISBN: 978-1-915951-20-5

ISBN: 978-1-911498-46-9

ISBN: 978-1-912555-57-4

ISBN: 978-1-912555-97-0